THE USBORNE PICTURE DICTIONARY IN GERMAN

Felicity Brooks and Fiona Chandler
Designer and modelmaker: Jo Litchfield

German language consultant: Barbara Bethäußer-Conte

Design and additional illustrations by
Mike Olley and Brian Voakes

Photography by Howard Allman

Contents

How to say the words

You can hear all the German words in this book, read by a German person, on the Usborne Quicklinks Website at **www.usborne-quicklinks.com** All you need is an Internet connection and a computer that can play sounds. Find out more on page 112.

Using your dictionary

You can use this dictionary to find out how to say things in German. Each page has 12 main words in English, with the same words in German (the translations).

The English words are in the order of the alphabet: words beginning with A are first in the book. There are also pictures to show what words mean.

This letter in a blue square shows the first letter of the English words on that page.

Don't forget that in a dictionary you read down the page in columns. In most other books you read across.

Short sentences or phrases, in English and in German, show you how the word can be used.

If you forget the order of the letters in the alphabet, look at the bottom of any page.

This word shows the first English word on the page.

This word shows the last English word on the page.

All the English words are shown in blue. The German translations are shown in black.

Sometimes the same English word appears twice with little numbers next to it. This shows that the same word can be used in two different ways. The German translations may look very different.

The blue letter also shows the first letter of the English words on that page.

S   start *to* stool

start   an/fangen*
The birds are starting to eat the seeds.
Die Vögel fangen an, die Samen zu fressen.

station   der Bahnhof
There are two trains at the station.
Es sind zwei Züge im Bahnhof.

stay (remain) bleiben, (visit) wohnen
The cows stay in the field.
Die Kühe bleiben auf der Weide.
He's staying at our house.
Er wohnt bei uns.

steep   steil
It's a steep path.
Es ist ein steiler Weg.

stick¹   der Stock, (from a tree) der Zweig
a big stick
ein großer Zweig
a walking stick
ein Spazierstock

stick²   kleben
Polly is sticking her picture on the wall.
Polly klebt ihr Bild an die Wand.

still¹   still
The car is standing still.
Das Auto steht still.
Milo is staying still.
Milo hält still.

still²   noch
Oliver's still hungry.
Oliver hat noch Hunger.
He still has some apples.
Er hat noch ein paar Äpfel.

sting   stechen
Bees can sting you.
Bienen können dich stechen.

stir   verrühren
Jack is stirring the mixture.
Jack verrührt die Mischung.

stone   der Stein
stones from the garden
Steine aus dem Garten

stool   der Hocker
a small, blue stool
ein kleiner, blauer Hocker

a b c d e f g h i j k l m n o p q r s t u v w x y z
* This is a separable verb (see page 99).

How to find a word

1 Think of the letter the word starts with. "Stone" starts with an "s," for example.

2 Look through the dictionary until you have found the "s" pages.

3 Think of the next letter of the word. Look for words that begin with "st."

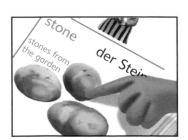

4 Now look down all the "st" words until you find your word.

2

Der, die or das?

In German, all nouns, or "naming" words such as "boy," "woman" and "house," are either masculine, feminine or neuter. The German word for "the" is *der* for masculine nouns, *die* for feminine nouns and *das* for neuter nouns.

You can sometimes guess whether a noun is masculine or feminine – for example, "boy" is masculine (*der Junge*). But some words are surprising – in German, "girl" is neuter (*das Mädchen*). So you should always check in the dictionary.

Finding a German word

All the German words in this book are listed at the back in the order of the alphabet. Can you put these fruits into alphabetical order?

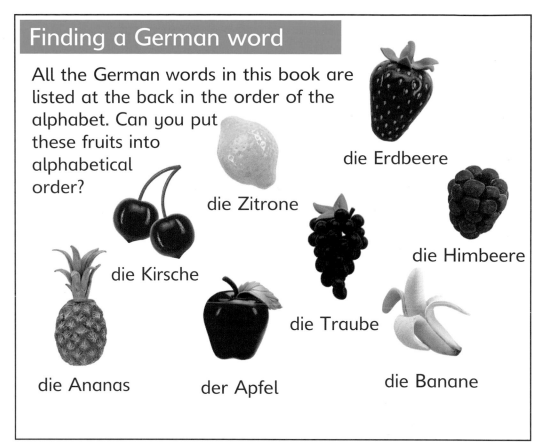

die Erdbeere

die Zitrone

die Himbeere

die Kirsche

die Traube

die Ananas

der Apfel

die Banane

Answer: die Ananas, der Apfel, die Banane, die Erdbeere, die Himbeere, die Kirsche, die Traube, die Zitrone.

Looking at a word

When you look up a word, here are some of the things you can find out.

You can check how to spell the word in English.

You can see how you might use the word in English and in German.

These words in parentheses show that you can use the word in different ways.

know (people) kennen,
(facts) wissen

Sam knows these children.
Sam kennt diese Kinder.

I know it's raining.
Ich weiß, dass es regnet.

If the word can be used in different ways, there are different phrases or sentences.

If the word can be used in different ways, there may be more than one German translation.

You can see a picture of the word, or a way of using the word.

Plurals

"Plural" means "more than one." The German for "the" when you are talking about more than one is *die* for masculine, feminine and neuter nouns. Usually, you need to change the spelling of the noun as well:

dog	der Hund
dogs	die Hunde
cat	die Katze
cats	die Katzen
house	das Haus
houses	die Häuser

You can see the plural spelling of all the words in this book in the German word list on pages 104 to 111.*

* In the word list, most nouns are written like this: *der Hund (-e)*. This means that the plural spelling of this word is *Hunde*. The plural spelling of some words is shown in full, like this: *das Haus (Häuser)*.

Nouns

In English, nouns always stay the same, no matter what part they play in a sentence. Look at the words "the dog" in these two sentences:

The dog sees Jack.

Jack sees the dog.

It doesn't matter whether the dog is seeing or being seen, its spelling doesn't change. German is different:

Der Hund sieht Jack.

Jack sieht den Hund.

Can you see how the word *der* changes to *den*? In German, the word for "the" (*der*, *die* or *das*) often changes depending on what part a noun plays in a sentence. The same thing happens with the word for "a" (*ein* for masculine and neuter nouns, *eine* for feminine nouns):

A dog has four legs.
Ein Hund hat vier Beine.

Polly has a dog.
Polly hat einen Hund.

A few masculine nouns actually change the way they are spelled. The German word for "name" is *der Name*, but it often adds an "n" on the end:

Write down your name.
Schreib deinen Namen hin.

Here are some other nouns that do the same thing:

| Mr. | Herr |
| neighbor | der Nachbar |

Adjectives

"Describing" words, such as "small" or "expensive," are called adjectives. In German, when an adjective comes before a noun, you need to add an ending to it. You add "er" with masculine nouns, "e" with feminine nouns, "es" with neuter nouns, and "e" with plural nouns:

a big tree
ein großer Baum

a green jacket
eine grüne Jacke

a cute kitten
ein niedliches Kätzchen

new shoes
neue Schuhe

You will sometimes see other adjective endings. This is because the endings change depending on what part a noun and its adjective play in the sentence:

Renata is wearing a red coat.
Renata trägt einen roten Mantel.

If an adjective comes after the noun it describes, you don't need to add any endings:

The sky is blue.
Der Himmel ist blau.

This bed is comfortable.
Dieses Bett ist bequem.

A few adjectives, such as *rosa* (pink), never add any endings:

a pink dress   ein rosa Kleid
a pink door   eine rosa Tür

Verbs

"Doing" words, such as "walk" or "laugh," are called verbs. In English, verbs don't change very much, whoever is doing them:

I walk, you walk, he walks

In German, the endings change much more. Most verbs work in a similar way to the one below. The verb is in the present – the form that you use to talk about what is happening now.

to play	spielen
I play	ich spiele
you play*	du spielst
he plays	er spielt
she plays	sie spielt
it plays	es spielt
we play	wir spielen
you play*	ihr spielt
they play	sie spielen
you play*	Sie spielen

In the main part of the dictionary, you will find each verb listed in the "to" form. You can find out more about verbs on page 99. And on pages 100 to 103, you will find a list of all the verbs in the book.

* In German, you use the *du* form for one person, either a young person or someone you know very well. You use *ihr* for more than one person that you know very well. You use *Sie* for one or more people who are older than you, or that you don't know very well. It is more polite.

4

Aa

actor ***to*** *ambulance*

a

actor   **der Schauspieler**
die Schauspielerin

The actors are   Die Schauspieler
waving.   winken.

add   **(things) hinzu/fügen*,**
(numbers) zusammen/zählen*

Polly adds 8 and 2.
Polly zählt 8 und 2
zusammen.
Billy's adding some
blocks to his tower.
Billy fügt ein paar
Klötzchen zu
seinem Turm hinzu.

address   **die Adresse**

This is Oliver's address.
Das hier ist Olivers Adresse.

Oliver Esser
Wurststraße 34
54321 Schokostadt

adult   **ein Erwachsener**

Minnie is a
child. Her dad
is an adult.
Minnie ist
ein Kind. Ihr
Vati ist ein
Erwachsener.

(to be) afraid   **Angst haben**

Maddy
is afraid
of spiders.
Maddy hat
Angst vor Spinnen.

after   **nach**

Sacha slides down
after Suki.
Sacha rutscht
nach Suki
hinunter.

Sacha

Suki

afternoon   **der Nachmittag,**
(in the afternoon) nachmittags

three o'clock in the afternoon
drei Uhr nachmittags

(what) age?   **(wie) alt?**

What age
is Olivia?

Olivia

Joshua

Ben

Wie alt ist Olivia?

air   **die Luft**

Greta's balloon
goes up into
the air.
Gretas Luftballon
steigt in die
Luft.

alone   **allein**

Katie is alone in the bathtub.
Katie ist allein in der Badewanne.

alphabet   **das Alphabet**

abcdefghijklm
nopqrstuvwxyz

The alphabet has 26 letters.
Das Alphabet hat 26 Buchstaben.

ambulance
          der Krankenwagen

The ambulance
is empty.

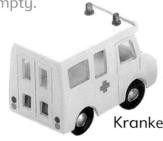

Der
Krankenwagen
ist leer.

a b c d e f g h i j k l m n o p q r s t u v w x y z

* This is a separable verb (see page 99).   5

amount	die Menge

a large amount of pasta
eine große Menge Nudeln

ankle	der Knöchel

Your ankle joins your leg to your foot.
Der Knöchel verbindet das Bein mit dem Fuß.

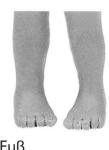

apple	der Apfel

An apple is a kind of fruit.

Der Apfel ist eine Obstsorte.

angel	der Engel

a Christmas angel

ein Weihnachtsengel

answer	die Antwort,
(to answer)	**antworten**

Question: Which animal says meow?
Answer: A cat.
**Frage: Welches Tier sagt miau?
Antwort: Die Katze.**

arm	der Arm

This is Jack's left arm.
Das ist Jacks linker Arm.

angry	böse

Jack is angry with Pip.
Jack ist böse auf Pip.

ant	die Ameise

Ants like sugar.
Ameisen mögen Zucker.

arrive	an/kommen*

The bus arrives at nine o'clock.
Der Bus kommt um neun Uhr an.

animal	das Tier

A lion is an animal.

Der Löwe ist ein Tier.

ape	der Affe

The ape is sitting on the ground.
Der Affe sitzt auf dem Boden.

art	die Kunst

This is Sam's picture.
He's good at art.
**Das hier ist Sams Bild.
Er ist gut in Kunst.**

a b c d e f g h i j k l m n o p q r s t u v w x y z

* This is a separable verb (see page).

artist der Künstler
die Künstlerin

The artist is painting some flowers.
Die Künstlerin malt ein paar Blumen.

baby das Baby

The baby is smiling.
Das Baby lächelt.

bag die Tasche,
(plastic, paper) die Tüte

all kinds of bags
allerlei Taschen

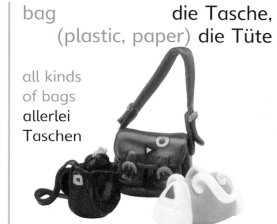

ask fragen

Becky is asking, "Can I have some more strawberries?"
Becky fragt: „Kann ich noch ein paar Erdbeeren haben?"

back¹ der Rücken

Polly is pointing to Jack's back.
Polly deutet auf Jacks Rücken.

bake backen

Oliver is baking some cupcakes.
Oliver backt etwas Gebäck.

(to be) asleep schlafen

Nicholas is fast asleep.
Nicholas schläft fest.

(at the) back² hinten,
(behind) hinter

He's at the back of the bus.
Er ist hinten im Bus.

baker der Bäcker
die Bäckerin

The baker sells fresh bread.
Der Bäcker verkauft frisches Brot.

astronaut der Astronaut
die Astronautin

Oliver is dressed up as an astronaut.

Oliver ist als Astronaut verkleidet.

bad schlecht, (naughty) frech,
(fruit, vegetables) faul

bad weather
schlechtes Wetter

a bad apple
ein fauler Apfel

a bad boy
ein frecher Junge

balance balancieren

The clown is balancing on one hand.
Der Clown balanciert auf einer Hand.

a b **c d e f g h i j k l m n o p q r s t u v w x y z**

(to be) bald — **eine Glatze haben**

Mr. Rogers is bald.
Herr Rogers hat eine Glatze.

banana — **die Banane**

A banana is a kind of yellow fruit.
Die Banane ist eine gelbe Obstsorte.

bar — **die Stange**

an iron bar
eine Eisenstange

ball — **der Ball**

a brightly colored ball
ein bunter Ball

band — **die Band**

Polly and Marco play in a band.
Polly und Marco spielen in einer Band.

bare — **nackt**

Marcus is all bare and ready for his bath.
Marcus ist ganz nackt und bereit für sein Bad.

ballerina — **die Balletttänzerin**

Lucy is a ballerina.

Lucy ist eine Balletttänzerin.

bang — **peng**

Bang! The balloon bursts.

Peng! Der Luftballon platzt.

bark¹ — **die Rinde**

the bark of a tree
die Baumrinde

balloon — **der Luftballon, (hot-air) der Ballon**

a pink balloon
ein rosa Luftballon

a balloon trip
eine Ballonfahrt

bank — **die Bank**

Mr. Brand goes to the bank to get some money.
Herr Brand geht zur Bank, um Geld abzuheben.

bark² — **bellen**

Pip is barking.
Pip bellt.

a b c d e f g h i j k l m n o p q r s t u v w x y z

barn   die Scheune

The barn is full of hay.
Die Scheune ist voll mit Heu.

base   der Fuß

The lamp has a yellow base.
Die Lampe hat einen gelben Fuß.

basket   der Korb

a big, round basket
ein großer, runder Korb

bat (animal) die Fledermaus,
(for sports) der Schläger

A bat isn't a bird.

Die Fledermaus ist kein Vogel.

a baseball bat
ein Baseballschläger

bathtub   die Badewanne

The bathtub is empty.
Die Badewanne ist leer.

beach   der Strand

They are playing on the beach.

Sie spielen am Strand.

beak   der Schnabel

A toucan has a big beak.
Ein Tukan hat einen großen Schnabel.

bean   die Bohne

green beans

grüne Bohnen

bear   der Bär

This bear has a brown coat.
Dieser Bär hat ein braunes Fell.

beard   der Bart

Mr. Brown has a beard.
Herr Brown hat einen Bart.

beautiful   schön

a beautiful pink cake
ein schöner rosa Kuchen

bed   das Bett

a comfortable bed
ein bequemes Bett

a b c d e f g h i j k l m n o p q r s t u v w x y z

bedroom *to* between

bedroom   **das Schlafzimmer**

Ben's bedroom   Bens Schlafzimmer

bee   **die Biene**

Bees make honey.
Bienen machen Honig.

beetle   **der Käfer**

Beetles have six legs.
Käfer haben sechs Beine.

beetroot   **die Rote Bete**

Beetroot grows
underground.
Rote Bete wächst
unter der Erde.

before   **vor**

Suki slides down
before Sacha.
Suki rutscht
vor Sacha
hinunter.

Sacha

Suki

begin   **beginnen**

Sam's beginning to fall asleep.
Sam beginnt einzuschlafen.

behind   **hinter**

The kitten is
behind the
flowerpot.
Das Kätzchen
ist hinter dem
Blumentopf.

belong   **gehören**

The book
belongs to Suzie.
Das Buch
gehört Suzie.

The CD
belongs to me.
Die CD
gehört mir.

below   **unter**

The kitten is below
the boards.

Das Kätzchen ist
unter den Brettern.

belt   **der Gürtel**

a brown belt
ein brauner Gürtel

beside   **neben**

The kitten is beside
the flowerpot.

Das
Kätzchen
ist neben
dem Blumentopf.

between   **zwischen**

The kitten is between
the flowerpots.

Das Kätzchen ist zwischen
den Blumentöpfen.

a **b** c d e f g h i j k l m n o p q r s t u v w x y z

10

bib — das Lätzchen

The bib has a duck on it.
Das Lätzchen hat
eine Ente
darauf.

bicycle — das Fahrrad

a blue bicycle — ein blaues Fahrrad

big — groß

a big elephant — ein großer Elefant

bird — der Vogel

All birds have wings.

Alle Vögel
haben Flügel.

birthday — der Geburtstag

a birthday party
eine Geburtstagsfeier

bite — beißen

Jon is biting
into an
apple.
Jon beißt
in einen
Apfel.

blanket — die Decke

a warm blanket
eine warme Decke

blow — blasen

Polly is
blowing out
the candles.
Polly bläst
die Kerzen aus.

boat — das Boot

a rowboat
ein Ruderboot

body — der Körper

some parts
of the body
einige
Körperteile

arm
der Arm

tummy
der Bauch

leg
das Bein

foot
der Fuß

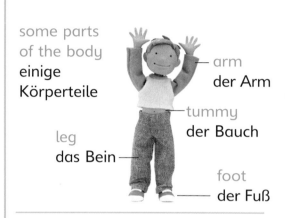

bone — der Knochen

How many bones
does Patch have?

Wie viele Knochen
hat Patch?

book — das Buch

Tina is reading a book.
Tina liest ein Buch.

a b c d e f g h i j k l m n o p q r s t u v w x y z

boot	der Stiefel

Alex wears boots when it's raining.

Alex trägt Stiefel, wenn es regnet.

bottle	die Flasche

a bottle of ketchup
eine Flasche Ketchup

a bottle of water
eine Flasche Wasser

bottom¹	der Po

Jack's bottom is inside the hoop.

Jacks Po ist im Reifen.

(at the) bottom²	unten

The kitten is at the bottom of the stairs.

Das Kätzchen ist unten an der Treppe.

bowl	die Schüssel

a plastic bowl   eine Plastikschüssel

box	(big) die Kiste, (small) die Schachtel, (cardboard) der Karton

The box is open.
Der Karton ist offen.

boy	der Junge

Oliver and Robert are boys.

Oliver und Robert sind Jungen.

branch	der Zweig

two birds on a branch

zwei Vögel auf einem Zweig

brave	tapfer

Mr. Sparks is very brave.
Herr Sparks ist sehr tapfer.

bread	das Brot

a fresh loaf of bread
ein frisches Brot

break	brechen, zerbrechen, (machine) kaputt/machen*

Asha has broken the vase.
Asha hat die Vase zerbrochen.

I've broken my radio.
Ich habe mein Radio kaputt-gemacht.

breakfast	das Frühstück

a healthy breakfast
ein gesundes Frühstück

a b c d e f g h i j k l m n o p q r s t u v w x y z

*This is a separable verb (see page 99).

breathe atmen

Divers breathe underwater.

Taucher atmen unter Wasser.

bridge die Brücke

The bus is driving over the bridge.
Der Bus fährt über die Brücke.

bright (light) hell, (color) knall-

a bright yellow car
ein knallgelbes Auto

The lamp makes the room bright.
Die Lampe macht das Zimmer hell.

bring bringen

Jack is bringing his letter to the mailbox.
Jack bringt seinen Brief zum Briefkasten.

brush die Bürste

a hairbrush and a toothbrush
eine Haarbürste und eine Zahnbürste

bucket der Eimer

buckets and shovels
Eimer und Schaufeln

bug der Käfer

These bugs are crawling around.

Diese Käfer krabbeln herum.

build bauen

Billy is building a tower.
Billy baut einen Turm.

building das Gebäude

This building has ten floors.
Dieses Gebäude hat zehn Stockwerke.

bump stoßen

Mr. Bun is bumping into the dog.
Herr Bun stößt gegen den Hund.

burger der Hamburger

a burger with cheese
ein Hamburger mit Käse

burn brennen, verbrennen, (food) anbrennen lassen

Dad has burned the burgers.
Vati hat die Hamburger anbrennen lassen.

a b c d e f g h i j k l m n o p q r s t u v w x y z

bus — der Bus

The bus is going into town.
Der Bus fährt in die Stadt.

bush — der Busch

Bushes are smaller than trees.
Büsche sind kleiner als Bäume.

a tree
ein Baum

a bush
ein Busch

busy — beschäftigt

Mr. Bun is busy in the kitchen.
Herr Bun ist in der Küche beschäftigt.

butcher — der Metzger

Mrs. Beef works at the butcher's shop.

Frau Beef arbeitet beim Metzger.

butter — die Butter

some butter for my bread

etwas Butter für mein Brot

butterfly — der Schmetterling

Butterflies are insects.

Schmetterlinge sind Insekten.

button — der Knopf

four brightly colored buttons

vier bunte Knöpfe

buy — kaufen

Suzie is buying an apple.

Suzie kauft einen Apfel.

café — das Café

Suzie and her dad are having breakfast at the café.
Suzie und ihr Vati frühstücken im Café.

cage — der Käfig

a small cage — ein kleiner Käfig

cake — der Kuchen

a delicious cake
ein leckerer Kuchen

calf — das Kalb

a cow and her calf
eine Kuh und ihr Kalb

a b c d e f g h i j k l m n o p q r s t u v w x y z

call *to* castle

call (to shout) **rufen**, (to name) **nennen**

Alex is calling Pip. **Alex ruft Pip.**

Komm, Pip!

Polly calls her doll "Caroline." **Polly nennt ihre Puppe „Caroline".**

camel **das Kamel**

Camels live in the desert.

Kamele leben in der Wüste.

camera **der Fotoapparat**

a new camera **ein neuer Fotoapparat**

camp **zelten**

They are camping. **Sie zelten.**

candle **die Kerze**

a cake with eight candles **ein Kuchen mit acht Kerzen**

cap **die Mütze**

a baseball cap **eine Baseballmütze**

car **das Auto, der Wagen**

a sports car **ein Sportwagen**

card **die Karte**

three birthday cards **drei Geburtstagskarten**

carpet **der Teppichboden,** (rug) **der Teppich**

My room has blue carpet.

Mein Zimmer hat einen blauen Teppichboden.

carrot **die Karotte**

A carrot is a kind of vegetable.

Die Karotte ist eine Gemüsesorte.

carry **tragen**

Aggie is carrying some flowers. Aggie trägt ein paar Blumen.

castle **das Schloss, die Burg**

an old castle **eine alte Burg**

a b c d e f g h i j k l m n o p q r s t u v w x y z

cat *to* cheap

cat   **die Katze**

The cat is licking its paw.
Die Katze leckt sich die Pfote.

catch   **fangen**

Jack is catching the ball.
Jack fängt den Ball.

caterpillar   **die Raupe**

two caterpillars
zwei Raupen

cauliflower   **der Blumenkohl**

a fresh cauliflower   ein frischer Blumenkohl

cave   **die Höhle**

There's a bear in this cave.
In dieser Höhle ist ein Bär.

CD   **die CD**

my favorite CD
meine Lieblings-CD

(in the) center   **mitten**

The fruit is in the center of the table.   Das Obst ist mitten auf dem Tisch.

the town center   die Stadtmitte

cereal   **die Getreideflocken**

I eat cereal for my breakfast.
Ich esse Getreideflocken zum Frühstück.

chair   **der Stuhl**

a small, blue chair
ein kleiner, blauer Stuhl

chalk   **die Kreide**

a chalk drawing
eine Kreidezeichnung

chase   **jagen**

Polly and Jack are chasing the dogs.
Polly und Jack jagen die Hunde.

cheap   **billig**

Everything is cheap in this store.
Alles ist billig in diesem Geschäft.

a b c d e f g h i j k l m n o p q r s t u v w x y z

cheese   der Käse

Swiss cheese
Schweizer Käse

chicken   das Hähnchen

I like roast chicken.

Ich mag Brathähnchen.

choose   wählen, aus/suchen*

Billy is choosing between the apple and the cupcake.
Billy wählt zwischen dem Apfel und dem Kuchen.

---

chef   der Koch
die Köchin

Mr. Cook is a chef.
Herr Cook ist Koch.

child   das Kind

three children   drei Kinder

city   die Großstadt, die Stadt

There are lots of buildings in a city.
Es gibt viele Gebäude in einer Großstadt.

the city of Berlin   die Stadt Berlin

---

cherry   die Kirsche

red cherries
rote Kirschen

chin   das Kinn

Jack's chin   Jacks Kinn

class   die Klasse

Mr. Levy's class
Herr Levys Klasse

---

chick   das Küken

This hen has five chicks.

Diese Henne hat fünf Küken.

chocolate   die Schokolade

a chocolate bar
eine Tafel Schokolade

classroom   das Klassenzimmer

our classroom   unser Klassenzimmer

a b **c** d e f g h i j k l m n o p q r s t u v w x y z

clean¹   putzen

Clean the glass!   Putz die Scheibe!

clean²   sauber

Neil's clothes are clean.
Neils Kleider sind sauber.

climb   hinauf/steigen*

Mr. Sparks is climbing the ladder to rescue the cat.
Herr Sparks steigt die Leiter hinauf, um die Katze zu retten.

clock   die Uhr, (alarm clock) der Wecker

My alarm clock is very noisy.
Mein Wecker ist sehr laut.

close¹   schließen, zu/machen*

Danny is closing the door.
Danny schließt die Tür *or* Danny macht die Tür zu.

close²   nahe, in der Nähe

Bill is standing close to Ben.
Bill steht nahe bei Ben.

The post office is really close.
Die Post ist ganz in der Nähe.

clothes   die Kleider

new clothes

neue Kleider

cloud   die Wolke

a big, white cloud
eine große, weiße Wolke

clown   der Clown

Look, the clown is juggling.
Schau mal, der Clown jongliert.

coat   der Mantel

Renata is wearing a red coat.
Renata trägt einen roten Mantel.

coffee   der Kaffee

Coffee has a strong taste.   Kaffee hat einen starken Geschmack.

coin   die Münze

Pete has two coins in his hand.
Pete hat zwei Münzen in der Hand.

a b c d e f g h i j k l m n o p q r s t u v w x y z

cold *to* crash

cold¹   die Erkältung, der Schnupfen

Helen has a cold.
Helen hat eine Erkältung.

come   kommen

The clown is coming to my party.
Der Clown kommt zu meiner Party.

country¹   das Land

The map shows the countries of Africa.
Die Karte zeigt die Länder von Afrika.

cold²   kalt

It's cold today. Ash is wearing his gloves.

Es ist kalt heute. Ash trägt seine Handschuhe.

computer   der Computer

a new computer
ein neuer Computer

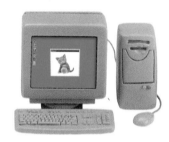

country²   das Land

springtime in the country

Frühling auf dem Land

color   die Farbe

bright colors   bunte Farben

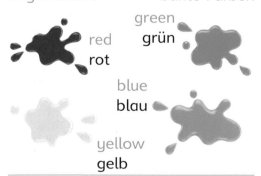

red   rot
green   grün
blue   blau
yellow   gelb

cook   kochen

Dad loves cooking.
Vati kocht sehr gern.

cow   die Kuh

Cows give milk.
Kühe geben Milch.

comb   der Kamm

a plastic comb
ein Plastikkamm

copy (actions) nach/ahmen*, (writing) ab/schreiben*

Sally's copying what Polly's doing.
Sally ahmt nach, was Polly macht.

crash   gegen . . . fahren, einen Unfall haben

The car has crashed into the tree.
Das Auto ist gegen den Baum gefahren.
Dad has crashed the car.
Vati hat einen Autounfall gehabt.

a b c d e f g h i j k l m n o p q r s t u v w x y z

crawl — kriechen, (baby) krabbeln

This baby is crawling. — Dieses Baby krabbelt.

Crawl through here! — Kriech hier durch!

crayon — der Wachsmalstift

a box of crayons — eine Schachtel Wachsmalstifte

creep — schleichen

Anna is creeping into the kitchen. — Anna schleicht in die Küche.

crocodile — das Krokodil

Crocodiles live near water. — Krokodile leben nahe am Wasser.

cross¹ — das Kreuz

A cross is made up of two lines.

Ein Kreuz besteht aus zwei Linien.

cross² — überqueren

a good place to cross the street

eine gute Stelle, um die Straße zu überqueren

crown — die Krone

Kings and queens wear crowns. — Könige und Königinnen tragen Kronen.

cry — weinen

Ross is crying. — Ross weint.

cucumber — die Gurke

some slices of cucumber

ein paar Scheiben Gurke

cup — die Tasse

a green cup — eine grüne Tasse

cut — schneiden, (cut out) aus/schneiden*

Danny is cutting a circle. — Cut the apple into four pieces.

Danny schneidet einen Kreis aus. — Schneide den Apfel in vier Teile.

cycle — mit dem Rad fahren

Sara cycles to school. — Sara fährt mit dem Rad zur Schule.

a b c d e f g h i j k l m n o p q r s t u v w x y z

* This is a separable verb (see page 99).

Dd dance *to* desk

dance — tanzen

Stef and Laura are dancing.
Stef und Laura tanzen.

day — der Tag

The sun rises every day.

Die Sonne geht jeden Tag auf.

delicious — lecker

Jack's sandwich is delicious.
Jacks Sandwich ist lecker.

dangerous — gefährlich

Some snakes are dangerous.

Manche Schlangen sind gefährlich.

dear — lieber *or* liebe

Liebe Julia,
vielen Dank für die Einladung zu deiner Party am 26. August.
Ich komme gerne.
Olivia

Lieber Philipp,
vielen Dank f... schöne Ges... du mir zum...

dentist — der Zahnarzt die Zahnärztin

The dentist is looking at Dad's teeth.
Der Zahnarzt sieht sich Vatis Zähne an.

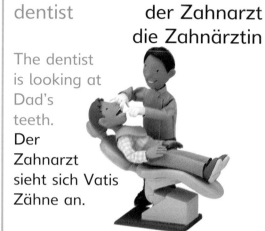

dark — dunkel

It's dark already.
Es ist schon dunkel.

dark blue
dunkelblau

deep — tief

a deep hole
ein tiefes Loch

desert — die Wüste

a hot, dry desert
eine heiße, trockene Wüste

date — das Datum

What's the date today?

Welches Datum haben wir heute?

deer — der Hirsch

This deer has big horns.
Dieser Hirsch hat ein großes Geweih.

desk — der Schreibtisch

My desk has six drawers.
Mein Schreibtisch hat sechs Schubladen.

a b c **d** e f g h i j k l m n o p q r s t u v w x y z

dictionary das Wörterbuch

A dictionary explains what words mean.
Ein Wörterbuch erklärt, was Wörter bedeuten.

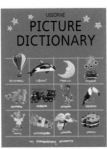

die sterben

My plant is dying because of the heat.
Meine Pflanze stirbt wegen der Hitze.

different verschieden

The twins wear different colors.

Die Zwillinge tragen verschiedene Farben.

difficult schwer, schwierig

It's difficult to take care of two babies at the same time.
Es ist schwer, sich um zwei Babys gleichzeitig zu kümmern.

dig graben

Anna is digging a hole.
Anna gräbt ein Loch.

digger der Bagger

a big, yellow digger   ein großer, gelber Bagger

dinner das Abendessen

Max is eating his dinner.
Max isst sein Abendessen.

dinosaur der Dinosaurier

an enormous dinosaur
ein riesiger Dinosaurier

dirty schmutzig

Sally's clothes are very dirty.
Sallys Kleider sind sehr schmutzig.

disappear verschwinden

Polly's dog has disappeared.

Pollys Hund ist verschwunden.

dive (into water) springen, (underwater) tauchen

Jack is diving into the water.
Jack springt ins Wasser.

I like going diving.
Ich gehe gern tauchen.

diver der Taucher

The diver is looking for coral.
Der Taucher sucht nach Korallen.

a b c **d** e f g h i j k l m n o p q r s t u v w x y z

do *to* dream

do — machen, tun

I have nothing to do.
Ich habe nichts zu tun.

Jenny is doing a jigsaw puzzle.
Jenny macht ein Puzzle.

doctor — der Arzt, die Ärztin

The doctor is taking care of Kirsty.
Der Arzt kümmert sich um Kirsty.

dog — der Hund

a nice dog — **ein lieber Hund**

doll — die Puppe

What's your doll called?

Wie heißt deine Puppe?

dolphin — der Delphin

A dolphin isn't a fish.

Der Delphin ist kein Fisch.

donkey — der Esel

A donkey looks like a small horse.
Ein Esel sieht wie ein kleines Pferd aus.

door — die Tür

The front door is red.
Die Haustür ist rot.

down — hinunter, herunter

This arrow points down.
Dieser Pfeil zeigt hinunter.

Come down!
Komm herunter!

dragon — der Drache

A dragon is a fairy-tale animal.
Der Drache ist ein Fabelwesen.

draw — zeichnen

Molly is drawing a face.

Molly zeichnet ein Gesicht.

drawing — die Zeichnung

Molly's drawing
Mollys Zeichnung

dream — der Traum, (to dream) träumen

Adam is having a strange dream.
Adam hat einen seltsamen Traum.

a b c **d** e f g h i j k l m n o p q r s t u v w x y z

23

d

dress *to* dull

---

dress¹ — das Kleid

Anya is wearing a red dress with white flowers.
Anya trägt ein rotes Kleid mit weißen Blumen.

---

dress² — an/ziehen*,
(yourself) sich an/ziehen*

I'm dressing my doll.
Ich ziehe meine Puppe an.

Robert is dressing himself.
Robert zieht sich an.

---

drink — das Getränk,
(to drink) trinken

Polly is drinking orange juice.

Polly trinkt Orangensaft.

a cold drink
ein kaltes Getränk

---

drive — fahren

Mick is driving a dump truck.

Mick fährt einen Kipper.

---

drop¹ — der Tropfen

two drops of water
zwei Wassertropfen

---

drop² — fallen lassen

Ellie has dropped her cake.
Ellie hat ihren Kuchen fallen lassen.

---

drum — die Trommel

a red drum   eine rote Trommel

---

dry¹ — trocknen,
(yourself) sich ab/trocknen*

Anna is drying herself with a blue towel.
Anna trocknet sich mit einem blauen Handtuch ab.

---

dry² — trocken

The laundry is dry.
Die Wäsche ist trocken.

---

duck — die Ente

There's a duck on the water.

Auf dem Wasser ist eine Ente.

---

duckling — das Entenküken

How many ducklings can you see?
Wie viele Entenküken siehst du?

---

dull — **(color)** matt,
(story) langweilig

dull green
mattgrün

a dull book
ein langweiliges Buch

---

a b c **d** e f g h i j k l m n o p q r s t u v w x y z

* This is a separable verb (see page 99).
24

Ee eagle *to* email

eagle der Adler

a big eagle
ein großer
Adler

ear das Ohr

Polly is pointing to Jack's ear.
Polly deutet auf Jacks Ohr.

early früh

Lucy is arriving
early at the
party.
Lucy kommt
früh bei der
Party an.

earth die Erde

The Earth
is our
planet.

Die Erde
ist unser
Planet.

easy leicht

$$l + l = ?$$

an easy math problem
eine leichte Rechenaufgabe

My book is easy to read.
Mein Buch ist leicht zu lesen.

eat (of people) essen,
(of animals) fressen

Oliver is eating
green apples.
Oliver isst
grüne Äpfel.

The dog is
eating a
biscuit.
Der
Hund
frisst
einen
Keks.

edge der Rand,
die Kante

The crayon is
on the edge
of the table.

Der Wachsmalstift
liegt am Tischrand.

egg das Ei

a boiled egg
ein gekochtes Ei

elbow der Ellbogen

Jack is pointing
to his elbow.
Jack deutet
auf seinen
Ellbogen.

electricity der Strom

A television can't
work without
electricity.
Ein Fernseher
kann ohne Strom
nicht funktionieren.

elephant der Elefant

an African elephant
ein afrikanischer Elefant

email die E-Mail

Polly is sending
an email.
Polly schickt
eine E-Mail.

a b c d e f g h i j k l m n o p q r s t u v w x y z

empty   **leer**

The cookie jar is empty.

Die Keksdose ist leer.

---

end   **das Ende**

The End

---

enjoy   (activity) . . . **gern***, (yourself) **sich amüsieren**

Molly enjoys singing.
Molly singt gern.
She's enjoying herself.
Sie amüsiert sich.

---

enormous   **riesig**

an enormous whale
ein riesiger Wal

---

envelope   **der Umschlag**

a pale green envelope

ein hellgrüner Umschlag

---

equal   **gleich**

The two girls have equal amounts of sand.

Die zwei Mädchen haben gleich viel Sand.

---

escape   **entkommen**

The black cat is escaping.
Die schwarze Katze entkommt.

---

even   **gerade**

The pink bunny is jumping on the even numbers.
Das rosa Häschen springt auf die geraden Zahlen.

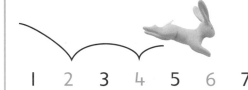

1   2   3   4   5   6   7

---

evening   **der Abend, (in the evening) abends**

The sun sets in the evening.

Die Sonne geht abends unter.

---

expensive   **teuer**

The duck is cheap, but the car is quite expensive.

Die Ente ist billig, aber das Auto ist ziemlich teuer.

---

explain   **erklären**

Mr. Levy is explaining the math problems.

$$2+3 =$$
$$5+4 =$$
$$8+5 =$$

Herr Levy erklärt die Rechenaufgaben.

---

eye   **das Auge**

Jack is pointing to Polly's eye.
Jack deutet auf Pollys Auge.

---

a b c d **e** f g h i j k l m n o p q r s t u v w x y z

* Add the word *gern* after the activity you enjoy doing: I enjoy swimming. **Ich schwimme gern.**

Ff face *to* feel

face¹   das Gesicht

This is
Jack's
face.

Das ist
Jacks Gesicht.

---

face²   gegenüber/stehen*

One giraffe
is facing
the other.

Die eine Giraffe steht
der anderen gegenüber.

---

fact   die Tatsache

Babies sleep
a lot – that's
a fact.
Babys schlafen
viel – das ist
eine Tatsache.

---

fairy   die Fee

The fairy has a
magic wand.

Die Fee
hat einen
Zauberstab.

---

fall   fallen, (over) hin/fallen*

Everyone
laughs when
the clown
falls over.
Jeder lacht,
wenn der
Clown
hinfällt.

---

far   weit

The butcher's shop isn't far away.

Die Metzgerei ist nicht weit weg.

---

farm   der Bauernhof

This farm has lots of sheep.
Dieser Bauernhof hat viele Schafe.

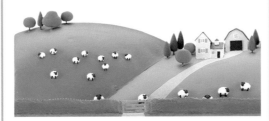

---

farmer   der Bauer

Mike is a
farmer.

Mike ist
Bauer.

---

fast   schnell

Eric goes very fast
on his skis.
Eric fährt sehr
schnell auf
seinen Skiern.

---

fat   dick, fett

a fat cat
eine dicke
Katze

a fat turkey
ein fetter Truthahn

---

feed   füttern

Polly is
feeding the
hens.

Polly füttert
die Hühner.

---

feel (touch) **fühlen, befühlen,** (happy or sad) **sich fühlen**

Feel this silk!
Befühl diese Seide!

Beth is
feeling great.
Beth fühlt
sich toll.

---

a b c d e **f** g h i j k l m n o p q r s t u v w x y z

* This is a separable verb (see page 99).

f

fence *to* first

fence — der Zaun

the garden fence
der Gartenzaun

few — wenige

Becky has very few strawberries.
Becky hat sehr wenige Erdbeeren.

field (for crops) **das Feld,** (for animals) **die Weide**

a field with cows in it — eine Weide mit Kühen darauf

a corn field — ein Kornfeld

fight — kämpfen, sich schlagen mit

The children are fighting with cushions.

Die Kinder schlagen sich mit Kissen.

fill — füllen

Ivan fills his wheelbarrow with sand.
Ivan füllt seine Schubkarre mit Sand.

find — finden

Megan is finding crayons under the table.

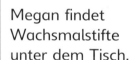

Megan findet Wachsmalstifte unter dem Tisch.

finger — der Finger

Jack is pointing to his finger.
Jack deutet auf seinen Finger.

finish — fertig machen, (to have finished) **fertig sein**

Danny has almost finished his juice.
Danny ist mit seinem Saft fast fertig.

Finish your work!
Mach deine Arbeit fertig!

fire — das Feuer

a wood fire
ein Holzfeuer

fire engine — das Feuerwehrauto

a model fire engine
ein Modellfeuerwehrauto

firefighter der Feuerwehrmann die Feuerwehrfrau

A firefighter puts out fires.

Ein Feuerwehrmann löscht Feuer.

first — zuerst, erst-*

Jenny is first.
Jenny kommt zuerst.

the first door on the left
die erste Tür links

a b c d e **f** g h i j k l m n o p q r s t u v w x y z

* You need to add an adjective ending to this word (see page 4).

fish¹   der Fisch

I have some tropical fish.
Ich habe ein paar tropische Fische.

fish²   angeln

Karl likes fishing.
Karl angelt gern.

fit¹   passen

This sweater doesn't fit Jenny.
Dieser Pulli passt Jenny nicht.

fit²   fit

Alice plays tennis to keep fit.
Alice spielt Tennis, um fit zu bleiben.

fix   (repair) reparieren, (attach) fest/machen*

Eve is fixing her doll.
Eve repariert ihre Puppe.

She is fixing the head on.
Sie macht den Kopf fest.

flag   die Fahne

the French flag
die französische Fahne

flat   flach

Mr. Clack holds the board flat.
Herr Clack hält das Brett flach.

float   (in water) schwimmen, (in air) schweben

The yellow duck is floating.
Die gelbe Ente schwimmt.

flood   die Überschwemmung

There are often floods here.
Hier sind oft Überschwemmungen.

floor   der Boden

The floor is covered in toys.

Der Boden ist voller Spielsachen.

flour   das Mehl

You need flour to make bread.
Man braucht Mehl, um Brot zu backen.

flower   die Blume

Roses are my favorite flowers.

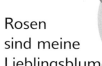

Rosen sind meine Lieblingsblumen.

a b c d e **f** g h i j k l m n o p q r s t u v w x y z

fly *to* freeze

fly¹ — die Fliege

A fly is an insect.
Die Fliege ist
ein Insekt.

fly² — fliegen

These two birds
are flying.
Die beiden Vögel
fliegen.

foal — das Fohlen

The foal is on
the left.

Das Fohlen steht links.

fold — zusammen/falten*

Clive is folding
the paper.
Clive faltet
das Papier
zusammen.

food — (prepared) das Essen, (groceries) die Lebensmittel

lots of food for the party

viel Essen für die Party

foot — der Fuß

Your foot is
at the end
of your leg.
Der Fuß ist
am Ende
des Beins.

forest — der Wald

a forest of fir trees
ein Tannenwald

forget — vergessen

Jan has forgotten the way.
Jan hat den Weg
vergessen.

fork — die Gabel

a blue fork
eine blaue Gabel

fox — der Fuchs

This fox has red fur.
Dieser Fuchs hat ein rotes Fell.

free — (no cost) kostenlos, umsonst, gratis, (not restricted) frei

You can get this honey free.
Diesen Honig gibt es umsonst.

KOSTENLOSER HONIG! FREE HONEY!

Is this space free?
Ist dieser Platz frei?

freeze — frieren, gefrieren, (food) ein/frieren*

You freeze water to make ice.
Man gefriert Wasser, um Eis zu machen.

It's freezing today.
Es friert heute.

a b c d e **f** g h i j k l m n o p q r s t u v w x y z

* This is a separable verb (see page 99). 30

freezer — der Gefrierschrank, die Tiefkühltruhe

The freezer is full.
Der Gefrierschrank ist voll.

fresh — frisch

All the fruit on this stand is fresh.
Das ganze Obst an diesem Stand ist frisch.

friend — der Freund, die Freundin

Ellie's friends are coming to her party.

Ellies Freunde kommen zu ihrer Party.

friendly — freundlich, lieb, nett

Marco is very friendly.
Marco ist sehr nett.

frog — der Frosch

This frog is from South America.
Dieser Frosch kommt aus Südamerika.

front — der (die, das) Vorder-*, die Vorderseite

The front door is open.
Die Vordertür ist offen.

the front of the house
die Vorderseite des Hauses

fruit — das Obst

some fresh fruit
etwas frisches Obst

fry — braten, (an egg) ein Spiegelei machen

Daddy is frying some eggs.
Vati macht Spiegeleier.
Can you fry the sausages?
Kannst du die Würste braten?

full — voll, (after eating) satt

Greg's shopping cart is full.
Gregs Einkaufswagen ist voll.

I'm full.
Ich bin satt.

fun — der Spaß

It's fun playing on the merry-go-round.

Es macht Spaß, auf dem Karussell zu spielen.

funny — (amusing) lustig, (strange) komisch

Jack is telling a funny story.
Jack erzählt eine lustige Geschichte.

a funny smell
ein komischer Geruch

fur — (on animals) das Fell, (on clothes) der Pelz

This kitten has soft fur.
Dieses Kätzchen hat ein weiches Fell.

a fur cap
eine Pelzmütze

a b c d e **f** g h i j k l m n o p q r s t u v w x y z

* You need to join this word onto the front of the thing you're describing: the front wheel – das Vorderrad.

game — das Spiel

a game of basketball
ein Basketballspiel

gentle — sanft

Pip is a gentle dog.
Pip ist ein sanfter Hund.

gift — das Geschenk

Becky has a birthday gift for Polly.

Becky hat ein Geburtstagsgeschenk für Polly.

garden — der Garten

There are lots of flowers in Aggie's garden.
Es gibt viele Blumen in Aggies Garten.

gerbil — die Wüstenspringmaus

A gerbil is a small animal.
Die Wüstenspringmaus ist ein kleines Tier.

giraffe — die Giraffe

A giraffe is an African animal.
Die Giraffe ist ein afrikanisches Tier.

gas — das Gas

This balloon is filled with gas.
Dieser Luftballon ist mit Gas gefüllt.

ghost — das Gespenst

I don't believe in ghosts.

Ich glaube nicht an Gespenster.

girl — das Mädchen

three girls — drei Mädchen

gate — das Tor

The garden gate is blue.
Das Gartentor ist blau.

giant — der Riese

a friendly giant — ein freundlicher Riese

give — geben, (as a gift) schenken

Ethan is giving Jenny some wagons.

Ethan gibt Jenny ein paar Waggons.

a b c d e f **g** h i j k l m n o p q r s t u v w x y z

(to be) glad — sich freuen

Sally is glad to see Jenny.
Sally freut sich, Jenny zu sehen.

glass — das Glas

Windows are made of glass.
Fenster sind aus Glas.

a glass of milk
ein Glas Milch

glasses — die Brille

Dad and Granny wear glasses.
Vati und Oma tragen eine Brille.

glove — der Handschuh

Polly has a pair of red gloves.
Polly hat ein Paar rote
Handschuhe.

glue — der Klebstoff

Danny is making a picture with
paper and glue.
Danny macht
ein Bild aus
Papier und
Klebstoff.

go — (on foot) gehen, (by car, boat, train) fahren

The cars are going into the ferry.

Die Autos fahren in die
Fähre hinein.

goal — das Tor

Our team has scored a goal.
Unsere Mannschaft hat
ein Tor geschossen.

TOR!

goat — die Ziege

Goats climb hills
very well.

Ziegen
klettern
sehr gut
auf Berge.

gold — das Gold, (golden) golden

Gold is a
precious
metal.

a gold watch
eine
goldene
Uhr

Gold ist
ein Edelmetall.

good — gut, (well-behaved) artig, brav

a good meal
ein gutes Essen

Good work!
Gute Arbeit!

$3 + 3 = 6$ ✓
$2 + 5 = 7$ ✓
$8 - 6 = 2$ ✓
$4 + 1 = 5$ ✓

a good child
ein braves Kind

goodbye — auf Wiedersehen, (to say goodbye) sich verabschieden

Polly is saying
goodbye to
her friends.
Polly
verabschiedet
sich von ihren
Freunden.

Auf
Wiedersehen!

goose — die Gans

A goose is a bird with
a long neck.
Eine Gans ist
ein Vogel
mit einem
langen
Hals.

a b c d e f **g** h i j k l m n o p q r s t u v w x y z

grape	**die Traube**

a bunch of grapes
ein Bund
Trauben

ground	**der Boden**

Polly is looking at
ants on the ground.
Polly schaut sich
Ameisen auf
dem Boden an.

guess	**raten**

Can you guess what
Polly's present is?
Kannst du
raten, was Pollys
Geschenk ist?

---

grapefruit	**die Grapefruit**

I like grapefruit with sugar.
Ich mag Grapefruit mit Zucker.

group	**die Gruppe**

a group of children
eine Gruppe Kinder

guest	**der Gast**

Ellie is welcoming the
guests.

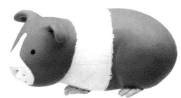

Ellie begrüßt die Gäste.

---

grass	**das Gras**

Cows and sheep eat grass.
Kühe und Schafe fressen Gras.

grow (get bigger) **wachsen,**
(cultivate) **ziehen**

My plant is
growing very fast.
Meine Pflanze
wächst sehr schnell.

We grow vegetables
in our garden.
Wir ziehen Gemüse
in unserem Garten.

guinea pig

das Meerschweinchen

a cute guinea pig

ein niedliches Meerschweinchen

---

great (big) **groß,**
(fantastic) **toll**

a great success
ein großer Erfolg

a great day
on the beach
ein toller
Tag am
Strand

grown-up	**der Erwachsene**

Grown-ups are always
stopping to talk.

Erwachsene
bleiben
ständig
stehen,
um sich zu
unterhalten.

guitar	**die Gitarre**

an electric
guitar

eine
elektrische
Gitarre

a b c d e f **g** h i j k l m n o p q r s t u v w x y z

hair   die Haare

Rosie and Katie have fair hair.

Rosie und Katie haben blonde Haare.

hairbrush   die Haarbürste

I have a red hairbrush.
Ich habe eine rote Haarbürste.

half   halb, (portion) die Hälfte

two-and-a-half hours
zweieinhalb Stunden

half the bun
die Brötchenhälfte

hamburger   der Hamburger

a hamburger with cheese

ein Hamburger mit Käse

hammer   der Hammer

a hammer for doing carpentry

ein Hammer zum Heimwerken

hamster   der Hamster

Hamsters eat nuts and seeds.
Hamster fressen Nüsse und Samen.

hand   die Hand

This is Jack's left hand.   Das ist Jacks linke Hand.

handle   der Griff, (door) die Klinke, (pan) der Stiel

the door handle   die Türklinke

The pan handle's broken.
Der Pfannenstiel ist kaputt.

hang   hängen

Jack is hanging his jacket up.
Jack hängt seine Jacke auf.

happen   passieren, los sein

What's happening here?
Was ist hier los?

happy   glücklich

Sally is feeling very happy today.
Sally ist heute sehr glücklich.

hard   (surface) hart, (task) schwer, schwierig

It can be hard putting up a tent.
Es kann schwer sein, ein Zelt aufzuschlagen.

The ground is hard.
Der Boden ist hart.

a b c d e f g **h** i j k l m n o p q r s t u v w x y z

hat   **der Hut**

an orange
hat with a
flower
on it

ein orangefarbener
Hut mit
einer
Blume
darauf

hear   **hören**

Jack can hear the
dog barking.

Wau! Wau!

Jack hört den
Hund bellen.

height (person) **die Größe,**
(house, mountain) **die Höhe**

We're flying at a
height of 30,000ft.
Wir fliegen in einer
Höhe von 9000m.

What height
is Milo?
Wie groß ist Milo?**

---

hate   **hassen,**
nicht leiden können

It's wrong to hate other people.
Es ist unrecht, andere Menschen
zu hassen.

Maddy hates
spiders.
Maddy kann
Spinnen nicht leiden.

heart   **das Herz**

My heart is beating fast.
Mein Herz schlägt schnell.

heart shaped
herzförmig

helicopter der Hubschrauber

a rescue helicopter
ein Rettungshubschrauber

---

have   **haben**

Julia has some
new red shoes.
Julia hat neue
rote Schuhe.

heat   (food) **auf/wärmen*,**
(a room) **heizen**

Yvonne is
heating her
coffee in the
microwave.
Yvonne wärmt
ihren Kaffee in
der Mikrowelle auf.

hello   **hallo**

Lisa is saying
hello to her
sister.

Hallo!

Lisa sagt
ihrer
Schwester
„Hallo!"

---

head   **der Kopf**

Polly's head is in the hoop.
Pollys Kopf ist im Reifen.

heavy   **schwer**

The package
is too
heavy.

Das Paket ist zu schwer.

helmet   **der Helm**

Grace wears a helmet
for skateboarding.
Grace trägt
einen Helm beim
Skateboardfahren.

---

a b c d e f g **h** i j k l m n o p q r s t u v w x y z

help *to* honey

help   helfen

Jack is helping his dad with the cooking.
Jack hilft seinem Vati beim Kochen.

hen   das Huhn, die Henne

Hens lay eggs.

Hühner legen Eier.

hide   (things) verstecken, (yourself) sich verstecken

The clown is hiding behind the armchair.
Der Clown versteckt sich hinter dem Sessel.

high   hoch, (before a noun) hoh-*

The balloon is floating high in the sky.
Der Ballon schwebt hoch am Himmel.

a high building
ein hohes Gebäude

highchair   der Hochstuhl

Highchairs are for small children.
Hochstühle sind für kleine Kinder.

hill   der Hügel

Our house is at the top of a hill.
Unser Haus ist oben auf einem Hügel.

hippopotamus *or* hippo   das Nilpferd

Hippos live in Africa.

Nilpferde leben in Afrika.

hit   schlagen

Alice is hitting the ball with her racket.
Alice schlägt den Ball mit ihrem Schläger.

hold   halten

Neil is holding the trophy.
Neil hält den Pokal.

hole   das Loch

This sweater has a hole in it.
Dieser Pulli hat ein Loch.

home   das Haus, (at home) zu Hause

This is our home.

Das ist unser Haus.

honey   der Honig

Honey is very sweet.
Honig ist sehr süß.

a b c d e f g **h** i j k l m n o p q r s t u v w x y z

* You need to add an adjective ending to this word (see page 4).

h

hop *to* hurt

hop   **hüpfen**

Anna is hopping on one leg.

Anna hüpft auf einem Bein.

horse   **das Pferd**

Martin likes riding his horse.
Martin reitet gern auf seinem Pferd.

hospital   **das Krankenhaus**

the new hospital
das neue Krankenhaus

hot   **heiß**

Careful, the stove's hot!

Vorsicht, der Herd ist heiß!

hotdog   **der Hotdog**

A hotdog is a sausage in a bun.
Ein Hotdog ist eine Wurst in einem Brötchen.

hotel   **das Hotel**

Mr. Brand is spending his vacation at this hotel.
Herr Brand verbringt seinen Urlaub in diesem Hotel.

HOTEL LUCIDA

hour   **die Stunde**

The short hand on the clock shows the hours.
Der kurze Zeiger auf der Uhr zeigt die Stunden an.

house   **das Haus**

a house with a yard
ein Haus mit einem Garten

hug   (person) **umarmen**, (toy, animal) **an sich drücken**

Nicholas is hugging his teddy bear.
Nicholas drückt seinen Teddy an sich.

(to be) hungry   **Hunger haben**

Oliver is hungry.
Oliver hat Hunger.

hurry   **sich beeilen**

Jack and Polly are hurrying to catch the dog.
Jack und Polly beeilen sich, um den Hund zu fangen.

hurt   **weh/tun***

Ross is crying because his tummy hurts.
Ross weint, denn sein Bauch tut weh.

a b c d e f g **h** i j k l m n o p q r s t u v w x y z

* This is a separable verb (see page 99).

Ii ice *to* itch

ice — das Eis

three ice cubes

drei Eiswürfel

ice cream — das Eis

different flavors of ice cream
verschiedene Eissorten

idea — die Idee

Gehen wir zum Park!

Andy has an idea: Let's go to the park!

Andy hat eine Idee.

insect — das Insekt

All insects have six legs.

Alle Insekten haben sechs Beine.

inside — in, (indoors) hinein, herein

There's a kitten inside this flowerpot.
Da ist ein Kätzchen in diesem Blumentopf.

Let's go inside.
Gehen wir hinein.

Come inside!
Komm herein!

instead (of) — statt

Ich habe heute Eistee statt Fruchtsaft gemacht.

Mrs. Dot has made iced tea instead of fruit juice today.

Internet — das Internet

Polly is searching the Internet.
Polly sucht im Internet.

invitation — die Einladung

a party invitation **eine Einladung zu einer Party**

Imogen lädt dich am Samstag, den 6. April um 16.30 Uhr zu ihrer Party ein.

invite — ein/laden*

Imogen is inviting Martin to her party.

Kommst du zu meiner Party?

Imogen lädt Martin zu ihrer Party ein.

iron — das Bügeleisen, (to iron) bügeln

a steam iron
ein Dampfbügeleisen

Dad is ironing his pants.

Vati bügelt seine Hose.

island — die Insel

a desert island
eine einsame Insel

itch — jucken

Fred's ear itches.
Freds Ohr juckt.

a b c d e f g h **i** j k l m n o p q r s t u v w x y z

* This is a separable verb (see page 99).

39

 # Jj   jacket *to* jungle

jacket   die Jacke

Kathy is wearing a yellow jacket.
Kathy trägt eine gelbe Jacke.

job   die Stelle, der Job

I'm looking for a job.
Ich suche eine Stelle.

Aggie has a job. She is a gardener.
Aggie hat einen Job. Sie ist Gärtnerin.

juggle   jonglieren

The clown is juggling with some toys.
Der Clown jongliert mit ein paar Spielsachen.

---

jar   das Glas

jars of honey, mustard and jelly
Gläser mit Honig, Senf und Marmelade

join   (attach) verbinden, (become a member) Mitglied werden

Ethan is joining the wagons to the train.
Ethan verbindet die Waggons mit dem Zug.

I'm joining a club.
Ich werde Mitglied in einem Klub.

juice   der Saft

a glass of orange juice
ein Glas Orangensaft

---

jeans   die Jeans

new jeans
neue Jeans

joke   der Witz

Jack's joke:
Jacks Witz:

Welches Tier macht sssb?

Eine Biene, die rückwärts fliegt!

What animal goes zzzub?
A bee going backward!

jump   springen

Sally is jumping in the air.
Sally springt in die Luft.

---

jigsaw puzzle   das Puzzle

This jigsaw puzzle is easy.
Dieses Puzzle ist leicht.

journey   die Fahrt, die Reise

a train journey
eine Zugfahrt

Have a good journey!
Gute Reise!

jungle   der Dschungel

There are lots of plants and animals in the jungle.
Im Dschungel sind viele Pflanzen und Tiere.

a b c d e f g h i **j** k l m n o p q r s t u v w x y z

kangaroo	kid	king
das Känguru	**das Zicklein**	**der König**

A kangaroo is an Australian animal.
Das Känguru ist ein australisches Tier.

a goat and her kid
eine Ziege und ihr Zicklein

Adam is dressed up as a king.
Adam ist als König verkleidet.

---

keep (store) **auf/bewahren*, (have) behalten**

kill **töten**

kiss **der Kuss, (to kiss) küssen**

Sam keeps his things on the shelf.
Sam bewahrt seine Sachen auf dem Regal auf.

Can I keep this book?
Kann ich dieses Buch behalten?

The heat has killed my plant.
Die Hitze hat meine Pflanze getötet.

Polly is kissing Alex.
Polly küsst Alex.

Give me a kiss.
Gib mir einen Kuss.

---

key **der Schlüssel**

kind[1] **die Sorte, die Art**

kitchen **die Küche**

the front door key
der Hausschlüssel

different kinds of fruit
verschiedene Obstsorten

The kitchen is on the ground floor.

Die Küche ist im Erdgeschoss.

---

kick **kicken**

kind[2] **nett, lieb**

kite **der Drachen**

Neil is kicking the ball.
Neil kickt den Ball.

Mr. Dot is kind. He does his neighbor's shopping.
Herr Dot ist nett. Er geht für seinen Nachbarn einkaufen.

a red and yellow kite
ein rotgelber Drachen

a b c d e f g h i j **k** l m n o p q r s t u v w x y z

kitten *to* know

Ll ladder *to* lake

kitten **das Kätzchen**

The kitten is playing with a ball of yarn. **Das Kätzchen spielt mit einem Wollknäuel.**

knee **das Knie**

This is Polly's right knee.

Das ist Pollys rechtes Knie.

kneel (be kneeling) **knien,** (kneel down) **sich hin/knien***

Suzie is kneeling. **Suzie kniet.**

knife **das Messer**

I need a knife to cut up the apple. **Ich brauche ein Messer, um den Apfel aufzuschneiden.**

knight **der Ritter**

This knight has a shiny suit of armor. **Dieser Ritter hat eine glänzende Rüstung.**

knock (on a door) **klopfen,** (over) **um/stoßen***

Pip has knocked the chair over. **Pip hat den Stuhl umgestoßen.**

knot **der Knoten**

a simple knot **ein einfacher Knoten**

know (people) **kennen,** (facts) **wissen**

Sam knows these children. **Sam kennt diese Kinder.**

I know it's raining. **Ich weiß, dass es regnet.**

ladder **die Leiter**

a small ladder **eine kleine Leiter**

lady **die Dame**

The two ladies are talking. **Die beiden Damen unterhalten sich.**

ladybug **der Marienkäfer**

A ladybug is an insect.

Der Marienkäfer ist ein Insekt.

lake **der See**

There is a small lake in the valley. **Im Tal liegt ein kleiner See.**

a b c d e f g h i j **k l** m n o p q r s t u v w x y z

* This is a separable verb (see page 99). 42

lamb *to* lean

L

lamb das Lamm

A lamb is a baby sheep.
Ein Lamm ist ein junges Schaf.

lamp die Lampe

Here are two table lamps.
Hier sind zwei
Tischlampen.

land das Land

On this map, the land is brown.
Auf dieser Karte
ist das Land
braun.

language die Sprache

¡Buenos días! Bonjour!

They can speak foreign languages.
Sie können Fremdsprachen.

large groß

a large tree
ein großer
Baum

last zuletzt, letzt-*

The black
dog is last.
Der schwarze
Hund kommt zuletzt.

last week letzte Woche

late spät

The bus always
arrives late.
Der Bus kommt
immer spät an.

I was late
for school.
Ich bin zu spät
zur Schule gekommen.

HAUPTSTRA 22

laugh lachen

Jack and Polly are laughing.

Ha! Ha! Ha! Hi! Hi! Hi!

Jack und
Polly
lachen.

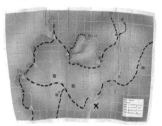

lazy faul

a lazy cat
eine faule Katze

lead führen, (go in front) voran/gehen**

The white duck is leading.

Die weiße Ente geht voran.

This road leads to the village.
Diese Straße führt zum Dorf.

leaf das Blatt

green leaves
grüne Blätter

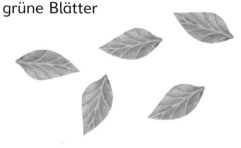

lean (lean on) sich stützen, (to one side) sich neigen

The tower leans
to the right.
Der Turm neigt
sich nach rechts.

Lean on
my arm.
Stütz dich auf
meinen Arm.

a b c d e f g h i j k **l** m n o p q r s t u v w x y z

* You need to add an adjective ending to this word (see page 4).
** This is a separable verb (see page 99).

l learn *to* lick

learn — lernen

Steve is learning to play the guitar.
Steve lernt, Gitarre zu spielen.

leave (a place) verlassen, (something) liegen lassen

Mr. Bun is leaving the house.
Herr Bun verlässt das Haus.

I've left my bag at home.
Ich habe meine Tasche zu Hause liegen lassen.

left — links, link-*

Turn left!
Geh nach links!
Lisa is holding the crayon in her left hand.
Lisa hält den Wachsmalstift in der linken Hand.

leg — das Bein

Tamsin wears tights to keep her legs warm.
Tamsin trägt eine Strumpfhose, um sich die Beine warm zu halten.

lemon — die Zitrone

seven fresh lemons

sieben frische Zitronen

length — die Länge

Use a ruler to measure the length of the paper.
Benutze ein Lineal, um die Länge des Papiers zu messen.

less — weniger

Ethan has less ice cream than Olivia.
Ethan hat weniger Eis als Olivia.

lesson — die Stunde

Mr. Levy is giving a math lesson.
Herr Levy gibt eine Mathestunde.

2 + 4 = 6

let — lassen

Mr. Dot is letting Jack mail the letter.
Herr Dot lässt Jack den Brief einwerfen.

letter — der Brief

a letter to a friend
ein Brief an eine Freundin

Eidorf, den 31. März

Liebe Anja,

vielen Dank für die schöne Tasche, die du mir geschenkt hast. Ich nehme sie jeden Tag mit zur Schule.

Liebe Grüße,

Olivia

lettuce — der Kopfsalat

a fresh head of lettuce
ein frischer Kopfsalat

lick — lecken, (animals) ab/lecken**

Pip is licking Jack.

Pip leckt Jack ab.

a b c d e f g h i j k **l** m n o p q r s t u v w x y z

* You need to add an adjective ending to this word (see page 4).
** This is a separable verb (see page 99).

lid der Deckel

the lid of the mustard jar
der Senfglasdeckel

lie¹ (be lying) **liegen,**
(lie down) **sich hin/legen***

Kirsty is lying in bed. Lie down!
Kirsty liegt im Bett. Leg dich hin!

lie² lügen

He's lying. Er lügt.

Sie ist nicht da? Nein!

life das Leben

Granny and Grandpa have had long, happy lives.
Oma und Opa haben ein langes, glückliches Leben geführt.

lift hoch/heben*

The clown is trying to lift the tree.
Der Clown versucht, den Baum hochzuheben.

light¹ das Licht

This lamp gives a lot of light.
Diese Lampe gibt viel Licht.

Turn off the light!
Mach das Licht aus!

light² (color) **hell,**
(not heavy) **leicht**

a light pink beach hut
ein hellrosa Strandhäuschen

This bag is really light.
Diese Tasche ist wirklich leicht.

like¹ (activities) . . . **gern****,
(people, things) **mögen**

I like playing tennis.
Ich spiele gern Tennis.
Becky likes strawberries.
Becky mag Erdbeeren.

like² wie

Sara has black hair, like her brother.
Sara hat schwarze Haare wie ihr Bruder.

line (on paper) **die Linie,**
(of people) **die Reihe**

a line of soccer players
eine Reihe Fußballspieler

Draw a line. Zeichne eine Linie.

lion der Löwe

Lions live in Africa.
Löwen leben in Afrika.

lip die Lippe

Zach's top lip
Zachs Oberlippe

a b c d e f g h i j k l m n o p q r s t u v w x y z

* This is a separable verb (see page 99).
** Add the word *gern* after the activity you like doing: I like singing. Ich singe gern.

list *to* lunch

list — **die Liste**	**long** — **lang**	**loud** — **laut**

list — **die Liste**

a list of first names
eine Liste mit
Vornamen

long — **lang**

A giraffe has a very long neck.
Eine Giraffe hat einen sehr langen Hals.

loud — **laut**

The music is too loud.

Die Musik ist zu laut.

live — (in a place) **wohnen**, (be alive) **leben**

The Dot family lives here.
Die Familie Dot wohnt hier.

look — **an/schauen***, **an/sehen***

Polly is looking at the clown.
Polly schaut den Clown an *or* Polly sieht den Clown an.

love — (people) **lieben**, (things) **sehr gern mögen**, (activities) . . . **sehr gern****

Beth loves her pink bathtub.
Beth mag ihre rosa Badewanne sehr gern.

lock — **das Schloss**

I need the key for this lock.
Ich brauche den Schlüssel für dieses Schloss.

lose — **verlieren**

I've lost my ticket.
Ich habe meine Fahrkarte verloren.

The boys have lost the match.
Die Jungen haben das Spiel verloren.

low — **niedrig**

This bird is flying very low.
Dieser Vogel fliegt sehr niedrig.

log — **der Baumstamm**, (for a fire) **das Holzscheit**

a log for the fire
ein Holzscheit fürs Feuer

(a) lot — (of one thing) **viel**, (of things) **viele**

a lot of water
viel Wasser

a lot of teddy bears
viele Teddys

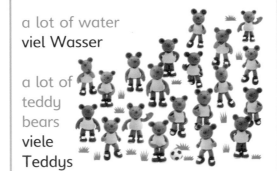

lunch — **das Mittagessen**

Sally is eating her lunch.
Sally isst ihr Mittagessen.

a b c d e f g h i j k l m n o p q r s t u v w x y z

* This is a separable verb (see page 99).
** Add the words *sehr gern* after the activity you love doing: I love dancing. Ich tanze sehr gern.

machine   die Maschine

a sewing machine

eine Nähmaschine

magic   die Zauberkunst, der (die, das) Zauber-*

The clown is doing a magic trick.
Der Clown macht ein Zauberkunststück.

a magic spell
ein Zauberspruch

main   der (die, das) Haupt-*

the main entrance of the museum
der Haupteingang des Museums

make   machen

Ethan is making potato people.
Ethan macht Kartoffelmännchen.

man   der Mann

This man has black hair.
Dieser Mann hat schwarze Haare.

many   viele

There are many bees on this flower.

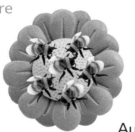

Auf dieser Blume sind viele Bienen.

map   die Landkarte, die Karte

a map of the region
eine Karte des Gebiets

market   der Markt

the fruit and vegetable market
der Obst- und Gemüsemarkt

match¹   (game) das Spiel, das Match, (for fire) das Streichholz

a soccer match
ein Fußballspiel

I have one match left.
Ich habe ein Streichholz übrig.

match² zusammen/passen**

These socks match.
Diese Socken passen zusammen.

These socks don't match.
Diese Socken passen nicht zusammen.

matter   wichtig sein

Winning matters a lot to Neil and his team.

Gewinnen ist für Neil und seine Mannschaft sehr wichtig.

meal   die Mahlzeit, das Essen

The meal is almost ready.
Das Essen ist fast fertig.

a b c d e f g h i j k l **m** n o p q r s t u v w x y z

* You need to join this word onto the front of the thing you're describing: a magic wand – ein Zauberstab; the main street – die Hauptstraße. ** This is a separable verb (see page 99).

mean — bedeuten

Mr. Levy is explaining what "x" means.
Herr Levy erklärt, was „x" bedeutet.

measure — messen

Dad is measuring Milo's height.
Vati misst, wie groß Milo ist.

meat — das Fleisch

Chicken is a kind of meat.
Hähnchen ist eine Fleischsorte.

medicine — das Medikament, das Mittel

cough medicine
ein Mittel gegen Husten

meet (by chance) begegnen, (by arrangement) sich treffen

I'm meeting Dad at six.
Ich treffe mich mit Vati um sechs Uhr.
Polly has met Lisa at the market.
Polly ist Lisa auf dem Markt begegnet.

mend — reparieren, (clothes) flicken

Robert is mending his shirt.
Robert flickt sein Hemd.

mess — das Durcheinander, (dirt) der Dreck

What a mess!
So ein Durcheinander!

message — die Nachricht

There's a message for Mom to call Paula.
Da ist eine Nachricht für Mutti:

Mutti, kannst du Paula anrufen?

metal — das Metall

This bucket is made of metal.
Dieser Eimer ist aus Metall.

microwave — die Mikrowelle

a new microwave
eine neue Mikrowelle

middle — die Mitte, (in the middle) mitten

The bear is in the middle of the grass.
Der Bär ist mitten auf dem Gras.

the middle of the town
die Stadtmitte

milk — die Milch

fresh milk
frische Milch

a b c d e f g h i j k l m n o p q r s t u v w x y z

mind — etwas gegen . . . haben, aus/machen*

I don't mind spiders.
Ich habe nichts gegen Spinnen.
I don't mind if it rains.
Es macht mir nichts aus, wenn es regnet.

minute — die Minute

It's a few minutes past nine.
Es ist ein paar Minuten nach neun.

mirror — der Spiegel

Jack's looking at himself in the mirror.
Jack schaut sich im Spiegel an.

miss — (train, bus) verpassen, (person) vermissen

Liddy misses her mom.
Liddy vermisst ihre Mutti.

Becky's missed the bus.
Becky hat den Bus verpasst.

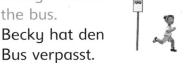

mistake — der Fehler

I've made a spelling mistake.
Ich habe einen Schreibfehler gemacht.

Giraffe
Hubschrauber
Marienkäfer
Schokolade
Zweig

mix — mischen, (cooking) verrühren

Oliver is mixing the ingredients to make a cake.
Oliver verrührt die Zutaten, um einen Kuchen zu machen.

model — das Modell

Billy has a model boat.
Billy hat ein Modellboot.

money — das Geld

I have some money to buy a present.
Ich habe etwas Geld, um ein Geschenk zu kaufen.

monkey — der Affe

five funny monkeys
fünf lustige Affen

month — der Monat

There are twelve months in a year.
Das Jahr hat zwölf Monate.

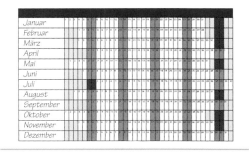

moon — der Mond

The moon is out.
Der Mond scheint.

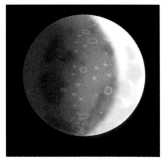

more — mehr

Sally has more sand than Amy.

Sally hat mehr Sand als Amy.

a b c d e f g h i j k l **m** n o p q r s t u v w x y z

* This is a separable verb (see page 99). It's also the other way around from English – as though you were saying "It doesn't bother me if it rains."

morning	der Vormittag, der Morgen

a summer morning
ein Sommermorgen

mountain	der Berg

Mountains are higher than hills.
Berge sind höher als Hügel.

much	viel

Mrs. Moon hasn't bought much.
Frau Moon hat nicht viel gekauft.

most	meist-*

Which caterpillar has the most stripes?

Welche Raupe hat die meisten Streifen?

mouse	die Maus

a house mouse
eine Hausmaus

a computer mouse
eine Computermaus

mud	der Schlamm

Sally is covered in mud.
Sally ist voller Schlamm.

moth	der Nachtfalter

Moths come out at night.

Nachtfalter kommen nachts heraus.

mouth	der Mund

Jack is pointing to Polly's mouth.
Jack deutet auf Pollys Mund.

mushroom	der Pilz

Mushrooms grow in fields and in woods.
Pilze wachsen auf Weiden und in Wäldern.

motorcycle	das Motorrad

This is Steve's new motorcycle.

Das hier ist Steves neues Motorrad.

move (yourself)	sich bewegen, (an object) um/stellen**

The crane is moving the crate.
Der Kran stellt die Kiste um.

Don't move! Beweg dich nicht!

music	die Musik

Steve, Marco and Molly love music.
Steve, Marco und Molly mögen Musik sehr gern.

* You need to add an adjective ending to this word (see page 4).
** This is a separable verb (see page 99).

Nn nail *to* nest

nail — der Nagel

I need some nails to fix the chair.
Ich brauche ein paar Nägel, um den Stuhl zu reparieren.

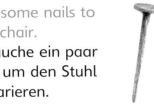

pink nail polish
rosa Nagellack

name — der Name*

Polly is choosing a name for her tiger.
Polly sucht einen Namen für ihren Tiger aus.

narrow — eng

The gap is too narrow – the kitten can't fit through.
Der Spalt ist zu eng – das Kätzchen kommt nicht durch.

nature — die Natur

Polly is interested in nature.
Polly interessiert sich für die Natur.

naughty — frech, unartig

That naughty dog has stolen Jack's cake.
Der freche Hund da hat Jacks Kuchen gestohlen.

near — in der Nähe von

The school is near the river.

Die Schule ist in der Nähe von dem Fluss.

neck — der Hals

A giraffe has a very long neck.
Eine Giraffe hat einen sehr langen Hals.

necklace — die Halskette

Ruth has a pretty necklace.
Ruth hat eine hübsche Halskette.

need (something) brauchen, (to do something) müssen

Sam needs to sleep. Sam muss schlafen.

I need a pencil. Ich brauche einen Bleistift.

needle — die Nadel

a sewing needle
eine Nähnadel

two red knitting needles
zwei rote Stricknadeln

neighbor — der Nachbar die Nachbarin

These two people are neighbors.
Diese zwei Leute sind Nachbarn.

nest — das Nest

Birds build nests for their eggs.
Vögel bauen Nester für ihre Eier.

a b c d e f g h i j k l m **n** o p q r s t u v w x y z

* You sometimes need to add an "n" on the end of this word (see page 4).

net¹ — das Netz

Julia has a small fishing net.
Julia hat ein kleines Fischernetz.

The ball's in the net.
Der Ball ist im Netz.

Net² — das Internet

Polly is searching the Net.
Polly sucht im Internet.

never — nie

The mailman never smiles.
Der Briefträger lächelt nie.

new — neu

Julia has some new shoes.
Julia hat neue Schuhe.

news — die Nachricht, das Neueste

Mrs. Beef has some bad news: her cat is gone!
Frau Beef hat eine schlechte Nachricht:

Meine Katze ist weg!

newspaper — die Zeitung

This is Dad's newspaper.
Das hier ist Vatis Zeitung.

next — (beside) neben, (after that) danach, (next week) nächst-*

The yellow car is next to the red car.
Das gelbe Auto ist neben dem roten Auto.

next year
nächstes Jahr

nice — (person) nett, (to look at) schön, (food) gut, lecker

Danny has made a nice picture.
Danny hat ein schönes Bild gemacht.

night — die Nacht

It's night time.
Es ist Nacht.

nod — nicken

The dog is nodding.
Der Hund nickt.

noise — das Geräusch, (loud) der Lärm

What's that noise?
Was ist das für ein Geräusch?

WAHH!

This baby is making a lot of noise.
Dieses Baby macht viel Lärm.

noisy — laut

The boys are very noisy.
Die Jungen sind sehr laut.

a b c d e f g h i j k l m **n** o p q r s t u v w x y z

* You need to add an adjective ending to this word (see page 4).

nose *to* nut

nose — die Nase

Polly is pointing to Jack's nose.
Polly deutet auf Jacks Nase.

note — (message) die Notiz, (music) die Note

a note for Mom to see the dentist at 10:30
eine Notiz für Mutti

notebook — das Notizbuch

This is Jack's notebook.
Das hier ist Jacks Notizbuch.

notice — bemerken

The clown is hiding and Annie hasn't noticed him.
Der Clown hält sich versteckt und Annie hat ihn nicht bemerkt.

now — jetzt

The clown is holding a pie . . .
Der Clown hält eine Torte . . .

. . . now he falls down in it.
. . . jetzt fällt er hinein.

number — (figure) die Zahl, (amount) die Anzahl, (street, phone) die Nummer

(981) 569-2636

Here's my phone number.
Hier ist meine Telefonnummer.

Two is an even number.
Zwei ist eine gerade Zahl.

nurse — die Krankenschwester

The nurse is pushing Sally in a wheelchair.
Die Krankenschwester schiebt Sally mit dem Rollstuhl.

nut — die Nuss

Nuts are good to nibble.
Nüsse sind gut zum Knabbern.

Oo ocean *to* odd — o

ocean — der Ozean

An ocean is a huge sea.

Ein Ozean ist ein riesiges Meer.

o'clock — Uhr

one o'clock in the afternoon
ein Uhr nachmittags

seven o'clock in the morning
sieben Uhr morgens

octopus — der Tintenfisch

An octopus has eight tentacles.

Ein Tintenfisch hat acht Fangarme.

odd — (number) ungerade, (strange) seltsam

The blue bunny is jumping on the odd numbers.
Das blaue Häschen springt auf die ungeraden Zahlen.

That's odd.   Das ist ja seltsam.

a b c d e f g h i j k l m **n o** p q r s t u v w x y z

often *to* other

often   **oft**

Mr. Dot and Jack often go and do the shopping.
Herr Dot und Jack gehen oft einkaufen.

oil   **das Öl**

Sunflower oil is good for cooking.
Sonnenblumenöl ist gut zum Kochen.

old   **alt**

an old woman
eine alte Frau

an old shoe
ein alter Schuh

once   **einmal**

They've been on a balloon trip once.
Sie haben einmal eine Ballonfahrt gemacht.

Once upon a time . . .
Es war einmal . . .

---

onion   **die Zwiebel**

Onions have a strong taste.
Zwiebeln haben einen starken Geschmack.

only   **nur, bloß**

Becky only has two strawberries.
Becky hat nur zwei Erdbeeren *or* Becky hat bloß zwei Erdbeeren.

open¹   **auf/machen*, öffnen**

Mr. Dot is opening the front door.
Herr Dot macht die Haustür auf.

Mrs. Dot is opening the box.
Frau Dot öffnet den Karton.

open²   **offen, geöffnet**

Mrs. Bird's store is open on Saturdays.
Frau Birds Geschäft ist samstags geöffnet.

---

opposite¹   **der Gegensatz**

"Big" and "small" are opposites.
„Groß" und „klein" sind Gegensätze.

opposite²   **gegenüber**

Becky is sitting opposite her teddy bear.
Becky sitzt ihrem Teddy gegenüber.

orange (fruit) **die Orange,** (color) **orangefarben**

a juicy orange
eine saftige Orange

orange paint
orangefarbener Lack

other   **ander-****

Hast du noch andere Spielsachen?

Äh...nein.

Jenny's asking if Ethan has any other toys.

---

a b c d e f g h i j k l m n o p q r s t u v w x y z

* This is a separable verb (see page 99).
** You need to add an adjective ending to this word (see page 4).

outside — draußen, außen, außerhalb

Let's play outside!
Spielen wir draußen!

The monkey is outside the box.
Der Affe sitzt außerhalb der Kiste.

over — (above) über, (finished) zu Ende

The bird is flying over the tree.
Der Vogel fliegt über den Baum.

The party is over.
Die Party ist zu Ende.

owl — die Eule

Owls come out at night.
Eulen kommen nachts heraus.

own — eigen

Mrs. Bird has her own store.
Frau Bird hat ihr eigenes Geschäft.

page — die Seite

Polly is looking at page 72.

Polly sieht sich Seite 72 an.

paint¹ — die Farbe, (on metal) der Lack

four bottles of paint
vier Flaschen Farbe

paint² — (picture) malen, (room) streichen

Shelley is painting a cat.
Shelley malt eine Katze.

I'm painting my bedroom blue.
Ich streiche mein Schlafzimmer blau.

pair — das Paar

a pair of striped socks
ein Paar gestreifte Socken

palace — der Palast, das Schloss

a palace with golden domes
ein Palast mit goldenen Kuppeln

pale — (face) blass, (color) hell, zart, blass

pale blue
hellblau

pale green
blassgrün

pale yellow
zartgelb

paper — das Papier, (newspaper) die Zeitung

some writing paper
etwas Schreibpapier

parachute — der Fallschirm

Mr. Brand is doing a parachute jump.
Herr Brand macht einen Fallschirmabsprung.

a b c d e f g h i j k l m o p q r s t u v w x y z

parents *to* pay

parents — **die Eltern**

Mr. and Mrs. Dot are Polly and Jack's parents.
Herr und Frau Dot sind Pollys und Jacks Eltern.

park¹ — **der Park**

Let's go and play in the park!
Gehen wir im Park spielen!

park² — **parken**

Jan parks in a parking lot.
Jan parkt auf einem Parkplatz.

parrot — **der Papagei**

Some parrots can talk.
Manche Papageien können sprechen.

part — **das Teil**

A wheel is part of a car.

Ein Rad ist ein Autoteil.

party — **die Party, die Feier**

There are lots of guests at Ellie's party.
Es gibt viele Gäste auf Ellies Party.

pass — (give) **reichen,** (go past) **vorbei/gehen***

They are passing the bank.
Sie gehen an der Bank vorbei.

Can you pass me the salt?
Kannst du mir das Salz reichen?

past¹ — **die Vergangenheit**

clothes from the past
Kleider aus der Vergangenheit

past² — **an . . . vorbei**

They run past the stores.

Sie laufen an den Geschäften vorbei.

path — **der Weg, der Pfad**

This path goes to the village.
Dieser Weg führt zum Dorf.

paw — **die Pfote**

This is the tiger's paw.
Das ist die Pfote des Tigers.

pay — **zahlen,** (for something) **bezahlen**

Who's paying?
Wer zahlt?

Ethan is paying for the apple.
Ethan bezahlt den Apfel.

a b c d e f g h i j k l m n o **p** q r s t u v w x y z

* This is a separable verb (see page 99).

56

pea — die Erbse

Peas are small, round vegetables.

Erbsen sind eine kleine, runde Gemüsesorte.

pear — die Birne

a sweet, juicy, green pear
eine süße, saftige, grüne Birne

penguin — der Pinguin

Penguins live in Antarctica.
Pinguine leben in der Antarktis.

peach — der Pfirsich

This peach is delicious.
Dieser Pfirsich ist lecker.

pebble — der Kieselstein

There are lots of pebbles on the beach.

Auf dem Strand sind viele Kieselsteine.

people — die Leute

These people are waiting for the start of the movie.

Diese Leute warten auf den Anfang des Films.

peak — (mountain) der Gipfel, (cap) der Schild, der Schirm

a snow-capped peak
ein schneebedeckter Gipfel

a cap with a peak
eine Schildmütze

pen — (ballpoint) der Kuli, der Kugelschreiber, (ink) der Füller

This is my new pen.

Das hier ist mein neuer Kugelschreiber.

pepper — (spice) der Pfeffer, (vegetable) die Paprikaschote

a pepper mill
eine Pfeffermühle

green, red and yellow peppers
grüne, rote und gelbe Paprikaschoten

peanut — die Erdnuss

a package of salted peanuts
eine Packung gesalzene Erdnüsse

pencil — der Bleistift

I'm drawing in pencil.
Ich zeichne mit Bleistift.

person — der Mensch, die Person

There is only one person here.
Es steht nur ein Mensch hier.

It costs two euros per person.
Es kostet zwei Euro pro Person.

a b c d e f g h i j k l m n o **p** q r s t u v w x y z

pet *to* pizza

pet	das Haustier

some pets
ein paar
Haustiere

phone	das Telefon

a yellow phone
ein gelbes Telefon

photo	das Foto

Polly is looking
at some
photos.

Polly sieht sich
ein paar Fotos an.

piano	das Klavier

I play the   Polly has
piano.   a toy piano.
Ich spiele   Polly hat ein
Klavier.   Spielzeugklavier.

pick (choose)	aus/suchen*,
(flowers, fruit)	**pflücken**

Oliver has   Oliver hat
picked an   einen Apfel
apple and   und einen
a cupcake.   Kuchen
                    ausgesucht.

I'm picking some flowers.
Ich pflücke ein paar Blumen.

picnic	das Picknick

Amy is having a picnic.
**Amy macht
ein Picknick.**

picture	das Bild

Shelley's painted a
very nice picture.
**Shelley hat ein
sehr schönes
Bild gemalt.**

piece	das Stück, das Teil

a piece
of cake
ein
Stück
Kuchen

a jigsaw puzzle with nine pieces
ein Puzzle mit neun Teilen

pillow	das Kopfkissen

a big, soft pillow
ein großes, weiches Kopfkissen

pilot	der Pilot / die Pilotin

Jim wants to
be a pilot.
**Jim will
Pilot werden.**

pineapple	die Ananas

A pineapple is a
kind of tropical fruit.
**Eine Ananas
ist eine
tropische
Obstsorte.**

pizza	die Pizza

a vegetarian pizza
eine vegetarische Pizza

a b c d e f g h i j k l m n o **p** q r s t u v w x y z

* This is a separable verb (see page 99).   58

place *to* pocket

place   die Stelle, der Ort, der Platz

Save me a place!
Halte mir einen Platz frei!

a good place to have lunch
ein guter Ort, um zu Mittag zu essen

---

plan¹   der Plan

a plan of the first floor

das Schlafzimmer

das Wohnzimmer

das Badezimmer

ein Plan des ersten Stocks

---

plan²   planen

Mrs. Dot is planning a party.
Frau Dot plant eine Party.

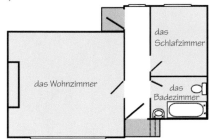

Datum: 22. Juni
Gäste:
Alex
Becky
Danny
Ellie

---

plane   das Flugzeug

The plane is landing.
Das Flugzeug landet.

---

planet   der Planet

a planet with rings
ein Planet mit Ringen

---

plant   die Pflanze

a potted plant
eine Topfpflanze

---

plate   der Teller

a clean plate
ein sauberer Teller

---

play   spielen

The children are playing outside.
Die Kinder spielen draußen.

Neil is playing soccer.
Neil spielt Fußball.

---

playground   (school) der Schulhof, (park) der Spielplatz

the playground in the park
der Spielplatz im Park

---

please   bitte

Becky is asking if she can please have some more strawberries.

Kann ich bitte noch Erdbeeren haben?

---

plum   die Pflaume

a nice, ripe plum
eine schöne, reife Pflaume

---

pocket   die Tasche

Renata is putting her hands in her pockets.
Renata steckt die Hände in die Taschen.

---

a b c d e f g h i j k l m n o **p** q r s t u v w x y z

poem	**das Gedicht**

Shelley has written a poem about her cat.
Shelley hat ein Gedicht über ihre Katze geschrieben.

Meine Katze
Meine Katze ist ganz weiß,
Ihr Schwanz ist lang
und ihr Fell ist weich.
Sie sitzt in der Sonne
und schnurrt und schläft,
Bis sie Hunger hat
und jagen geht.
Nachts kommt sie leise
in mein Bett,
Und wir schlafen
beide, bis Mutti
uns weckt.

point¹	(sharp) **die Spitze**, (score) **der Punkt**

the pencil point
die Bleistiftspitze

We're playing a game, and I already have forty points.
Wir spielen ein Spiel und ich habe schon vierzig Punkte.

point²	**deuten, zeigen**

Polly is pointing to Jack's nose.
Polly deutet auf Jacks Nase.

Don't point!
Zeig nicht mit dem Finger!

police	**die Polizei**

Brian works for the police.
Brian arbeitet bei der Polizei.

police car	**das Polizeiauto**

There is no one in the police car.
Niemand ist im Polizeiauto.

pond	**der Teich**

a duck pond
ein Ententeich

pony	**das Pony**

a small pony
ein kleines Pony

pool	**das Schwimmbad, das Schwimmbecken**

There's a children's pool in the park.
Im Park ist ein Kinderschwimmbecken.

poor	**arm**

rich people and poor people
reiche Leute und arme Leute

Poor Ross! He has a tummy ache.
Der arme Ross! Er hat Bauchschmerzen.

potato	**die Kartoffel**

Potatoes grow underground.
Kartoffeln wachsen unter der Erde.

present	**das Geschenk**

a surprise present for Polly
ein Überraschungsgeschenk für Polly

press	**drücken**

Danny is pressing down the blue paper with his hands.
Danny drückt mit den Händen auf das blaue Papier.

a b c d e f g h i j k l m n o **p** q r s t u v w x y z

pretend *to* puppet

pretend — tun als ob

Nicholas is pretending to be asleep.

Nicholas tut, als ob er schläft.

pretty — hübsch

Anya has a pretty red dress.
Anya hat ein hübsches rotes Kleid.

price — der Preis

The watermelons are two for the price of one.

2 zum Preis von 1

prince — der Prinz

a brave prince — ein tapferer Prinz

princess — die Prinzessin

a beautiful princess
eine schöne Prinzessin

prize — der Preis

Neil's team has won a prize.
Neils Mannschaft hat einen Preis gewonnen.

promise — versprechen

Ich nehme dich mit in den Park, ich verspreche es dir.

Minnie's dad is promising to take her to the park.

puddle — die Pfütze

Alex is jumping in the puddles.
Alex hüpft in die Pfützen.

pull — ziehen

Jack is pulling the package.

Thomas   Jack

Jack zieht am Paket.

pumpkin — der Kürbis

A pumpkin is a large fruit.
Ein Kürbis ist eine große Frucht.

pupil — der Schüler die Schülerin

Mr. Levy and his pupils

Herr Levy und seine Schüler

puppet — die Puppe, (on strings) die Marionette

This puppet is wearing funny clothes.

Diese Marionette hat komische Kleider an.

a b c d e f g h i j k l m n o p q r s t u v w x y z

puppy — das Hündchen

A puppy is a young dog.

Ein Hündchen ist ein junger Hund.

push — schieben

Thomas is pushing the package.

Thomas   Jack

Thomas schiebt das Paket.

put — (set down) stellen, setzen, legen, (put inside) stecken

Oliver is putting the bottle on the table.
Oliver stellt die Flasche auf den Tisch.

puzzle — (jigsaw) das Puzzle, (wordgame) das Rätsel

an easy puzzle — ein leichtes Puzzle

quack — quaken

Ducks quack.
Enten quaken.

Quak! Quak!

quarter — das Viertel

a quarter past three
Viertel nach drei

a quarter of the cake
ein Viertel des Kuchens

queen — die Königin

Joy is dressed up as a queen.
Joy ist als Königin verkleidet.

question — die Frage

Polly is asking a question: what's the clown called?

Wie heißt du?

Polly stellt eine Frage.

quick — schnell

Grace is very quick on her skateboard.

Grace fährt sehr schnell mit ihrem Skateboard.

quiet — leise, ruhig, still

Anna is very quiet – Milo doesn't hear her.
Anna ist sehr still – Milo hört sie nicht.

quite — (fairly) ziemlich, (completely) ganz

I'm quite tired.
Ich bin ziemlich müde.

Mr. Bun hasn't quite finished.
Herr Bun ist nicht ganz fertig.

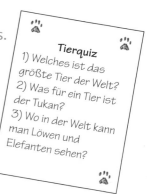

quiz — das Quiz

This is a quiz about animals.
Das ist ein Quiz über Tiere.

Tierquiz
1) Welches ist das größte Tier der Welt?
2) Was für ein Tier ist der Tukan?
3) Wo in der Welt kann man Löwen und Elefanten sehen?

a b c d e f g h i j k l m n o **p** **q** r s t u v w x y z

Rr rabbit *to* real

rabbit   das Kaninchen

Rabbits have long ears.
Kaninchen haben lange Ohren.

race   das Wettrennen

Polly and Jack are having a race.
Polly und Jack machen ein Wettrennen.

radio   das Radio

I'm listening to the radio.
Ich höre Radio.

rain   der Regen, (to rain) regnen

It's raining hard.

Es regnet stark.

rainbow   der Regenbogen

Look, there's a rainbow!
Schau mal, da ist ein Regenbogen!

raisin   die Rosine

I need raisins to make a cake.
Ich brauche Rosinen, um einen Kuchen zu machen.

raspberry   die Himbeere

These raspberries come from my garden.

Diese Himbeeren kommen aus meinem Garten.

rat   die Ratte

Rats are like mice, but bigger.
Ratten sind wie Mäuse, aber größer.

reach   heran/reichen*, (arrive) an/kommen*

The firefighter can reach the cat.
Der Feuerwehrmann kann an die Katze heranreichen.
The bus reaches the village at noon.
Der Bus kommt zu Mittag im Dorf an.

read   lesen

Tina is reading a book.
Tina liest ein Buch.

ready   bereit, fertig

The children are ready to go swimming.

Die Kinder sind bereit zum Schwimmen.

real   (not artificial) echt, (not imaginary) wirklich

That isn't real fruit, it's plastic.
Das ist kein echtes Obst, es ist aus Plastik.

in real life
im wirklichen Leben

a b c d e f g h i j k l m n o p q r s t u v w x y z

recorder   die Blockflöte

At school I'm learning to play the recorder.

In der Schule lerne ich, Blockflöte zu spielen.

refrigerator   der Kühlschrank

The refrigerator is full.
Der Kühlschrank ist voll.

remember   sich erinnern an

Fiona can remember the date of her friend's birthday.
Fiona kann sich an den Geburtstag ihrer Freundin erinnern.

> Du hast am 26. Mai Geburtstag.

reply   antworten

> Willst du in den Park gehen?

> Ja, bitte.

Minnie is replying to her dad.
Minnie antwortet ihrem Vati.

rescue   retten

Mr. Sparks has rescued the cat.
Herr Sparks hat die Katze gerettet.

rhinoceros   das Nashorn
or rhino

Rhinos live in hot countries.

Nashörner leben in heißen Ländern.

ribbon   das Band

Becky has green ribbons in her hair.
Becky hat grüne Bänder im Haar.

rice   der Reis

I prefer rice to pasta.
Ich esse lieber Reis als Nudeln.

rich   reich

Natalie is a very rich singer.
Natalie ist eine sehr reiche Sängerin.

ride   (horse) reiten, (bicycle) fahren

Martin is riding his horse.
Martin reitet auf seinem Pferd.

I like riding my bike.
Ich fahre gern Rad.

right   (not wrong) richtig, (not left) rechts, recht-*

That's the right answer.
Das ist die richtige Antwort.

Greta has the puppet on her right hand.
Greta hat die Puppe an der rechten Hand.

ring'   der Ring

a ring with a red stone
ein Ring mit einem roten Stein

the rings of Saturn
die Saturnringe

a b c d e f g h i j k l m n o p q **r** s t u v w x y z
* You need to add an adjective ending to this word (see page 4).

ring *to* round

ring² — klingeln, läuten

The phone's ringing.
Das Telefon klingelt.

Klingeling!

robot — der Roboter

a toy robot
ein Spielzeugroboter

room — (space) der Platz, (in house) das Zimmer

On this plan, there are six rooms.
Auf diesem Plan sind sechs Zimmer.

Is there room for me?
Ist hier Platz für mich?

ripe — reif

The melon, the avocado and the watermelon are all ripe.

Die Melone, die Avocado und die Wassermelone sind alle reif.

rock — (stone) der Fels, der Stein, (music) die Rockmusik

There are rocks on the beach.
Am Strand sind Felsen.
Steve likes playing rock music.
Steve spielt gern Rockmusik.

rope — das Seil

The rope is neatly tied.
Das Seil ist ordentlich gebunden.

river — der Fluss

The houses are by the river.

Die Häuser sind am Fluss.

rocket — die Rakete

a toy rocket
eine Spielzeugrakete

rose — die Rose

a red rose
eine rote Rose

road — die Straße

The road goes into town.
Die Straße führt in die Stadt.

roof — das Dach

This building has a blue roof.
Dieses Gebäude hat ein blaues Dach.

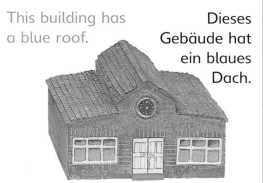

round — rund

Most drums are round.

Die meisten Trommeln sind rund.

a b c d e f g h i j k l m n o p q r s t u v w x y z

rug (big) der Teppich, (small) der Vorleger

a soft rug
ein weicher Teppich

ruler das Lineal

You can use a ruler to draw straight lines.
Mit einem Lineal kann man gerade Linien zeichnen.

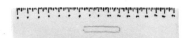

run laufen, rennen

Polly and Jack are running.
Polly und Jack laufen *or* Polly und Jack rennen.

rush (move quickly) eilen, laufen, (hurry) sich beeilen

They are rushing after Pip.
Sie eilen Pip hinterher.

sad traurig

Liddy is sad without her mommy.
Liddy ist traurig ohne ihre Mutti.

saddle der Sattel

Martin's horse has a new saddle.
Martins Pferd hat einen neuen Sattel.

safe sicher

a safe place to cross the street
eine sichere Stelle, um die Straße zu überqueren

sailor der Matrose, die Matrosin

Gareth is dressed up as a sailor.
Gareth ist als Matrose verkleidet.

salad der Salat

a mixed salad
ein gemischter Salat

salami die Salami

This is Italian salami.
Das hier ist italienische Salami.

salt das Salz

I've spilled the salt.
Ich habe das Salz verschüttet.

same gleich, (der-, die-,) dasselbe*

The twins always wear the same colors.
Die Zwillinge tragen immer die gleichen Farben.

a b c d e f g h i j k l m n o p q r s t u v w x y z

* You use *derselbe* with masculine words, *dieselbe* with feminine words, *dasselbe* with neuter words and *dieselben* with plural words: We go to the same school. Wir gehen auf dieselbe Schule.

sand — der Sand

The children are building sand castles.
Die Kinder bauen Sandburgen.

sandal — die Sandale

Where is the other sandal?
Wo ist die andere Sandale?

sandwich — das belegte Brot, das -brot*

a cheese sandwich
ein Käsebrot

saucer — die Untertasse

a cup and saucer
eine Tasse und eine Untertasse

sausage — die Wurst

a spicy sausage
eine würzige Wurst

save (from danger) retten, (time or money) sparen

Mr. Sparks has saved the cat.
Herr Sparks hat die Katze gerettet.

Jack is saving money in this bank.
Jack spart Geld in dieser Sparbüchse.

saw — die Säge

a saw for cutting wood

eine Säge zum Holzschneiden

say — sagen

Yvonne is saying, "Sleep well, darling."

Schlaf gut, Schätzchen!

Yvonne sagt: „Schlaf gut, Schätzchen!"

scarf — der Schal

I knitted this scarf.
Ich habe diesen Schal gestrickt.

school — die Schule

There are lots of children at this school.

Es sind viele Kinder an dieser Schule.

scissors — die Schere

These are safety scissors.

Das ist eine Sicherheitsschere.

scooter — der Roller, (with motor) der Motorroller

Shaun has a green scooter.

Shaun hat einen grünen Roller.

a b c d e f g h i j k l m n o p q r **s** t u v w x y z

* You need to add the type of sandwich onto the front of this word: a ham sandwich – ein Schinkenbrot.

sea　　　das Meer, die See

The sea is calm today.

Das Meer ist heute ruhig.

seal　　　der Seehund

Seals live by the sea.
Seehunde leben am Meer.

search　　　suchen

They are searching for their friend.
Sie suchen nach ihrem Freund.

seat　　(chair) der Sitz, (place to sit) der Platz

There are three seats free.

Drei Plätze sind frei.

secret　　　das Geheimnis

Amy is telling Anna a secret.
Amy vertraut Anna ein Geheimnis an.

see　　sehen, (visit) besuchen

Annie can't see the clown.
Annie sieht den Clown nicht.

I'm going to see my grandparents.
Ich gehe meine Großeltern besuchen.

sell　　　verkaufen

Mrs. Hussain is selling Ethan an apple.
Frau Hussain verkauft Ethan einen Apfel.

send　　　schicken

Jack is sending a letter to his friend.
Jack schickt seinem Freund einen Brief.

sentence　　　der Satz

This is a complete sentence.

My dad plays tennis.
Mein Vati spielt Tennis.

Das ist ein ganzer Satz.

sew　　　nähen

Robert is sewing his shirt.
Robert näht sein Hemd.

shadow　　　der Schatten

Look at Robert's shadow!
Schau mal Roberts Schatten an!

shake　　　schütteln

Anton likes shaking his rattle.
Anton schüttelt gern seine Rassel.

a b c d e f g h i j k l m n o p q r **s** t u v w x y z

shallow — seicht, nicht tief

The children's pool is shallow.

Das Kinderschwimmbecken ist nicht tief.

shampoo — das Shampoo

Can you lend me some shampoo? — Kannst du mir etwas Shampoo leihen?

share — teilen

Bill is sharing his cherries with Ben.
Bill teilt seine Kirschen mit Ben.

shark — der Hai

This shark lives in tropical seas.

Dieser Hai lebt in tropischen Meeren.

sharp — (edge) scharf, (point) spitz

Watch out! The knife is sharp.
Pass auf! Das Messer ist scharf.

This is a sharp pencil.
Das ist ein spitzer Bleistift.

sheep — das Schaf

Wool comes from sheep.
Schafe geben Wolle.

sheet — (of paper) das Blatt, (on bed) das Bettlaken

a white sheet
ein weißes Bettlaken

a sheet of writing paper
ein Blatt Schreibpapier

shelf — das Regal

Sam keeps his things on this shelf.
Sam bewahrt seine Sachen auf diesem Regal auf.

shell — (sea) die Muschel, (eggs, nuts) die Schale

I collect shells.

Ich sammle Muscheln.

an eggshell
eine Eierschale

ship — das Schiff

a cruise ship
ein Kreuzfahrtschiff

shirt — das Hemd

Milo is wearing a plaid shirt.
Milo hat ein kariertes Hemd an.

shoe — der Schuh

These are Robert's new shoes.

Das sind Roberts neue Schuhe.

a b c d e f g h i j k l m n o p q r s t u v w x y z

short   kurz

Maisie has short hair.
Maisie hat kurze Haare.

show   zeigen

Jack is showing Thomas his hands.
Jack zeigt Thomas die Hände.

Show me your picture.
Zeig mir dein Bild!

side   die Seite

I'm on your side.
Ich bin auf deiner Seite.

I write on both sides of the paper.
Ich schreibe auf beide Seiten des Papiers.

shorts   die Shorts, die kurze Hose

brightly colored shorts

bunte Shorts *or* eine bunte kurze Hose

shower   (rain) der Schauer, (for washing) die Dusche

Robert is in the shower.
Robert steht unter der Dusche.

sun and showers
Sonne und Schauer

sign¹   (road) das Schild, (symbol) das Zeichen

This sign means "no buses."
Dieses Schild bedeutet „keine Busse".

@ is the sign for "at."
@ ist das Zeichen für „bei".

shoulder   die Schulter

This is Jack's shoulder.
Das hier ist Jacks Schulter.

shrink   kleiner werden, (clothes) ein/laufen*

Wool clothes sometimes shrink in hot water.
Wollkleider laufen manchmal im heißen Wasser ein.

sign²   unterschreiben

The paper says "Sign here please."

Bitte hier unterschreiben

shout   rufen, (very loudly) schreien

HALT, PIP!

Jack is shouting, "Stop, Pip!"
Jack ruft: „Halt, Pip!"

shut   zu/machen*, schließen

Danny is shutting the door.
Danny macht die Tür zu *or* Danny schließt die Tür.

since   seit

They've been waiting since noon.
Sie warten schon seit Mittag.

a b c d e f g h i j k l m n o p q r s t u v w x y z

sing — singen

Molly can sing very well.
Molly kann sehr gut singen.

size — die Größe

This T-shirt is the right size for Zoe.

Dieses T-Shirt hat die richtige Größe für Zoe.

skirt — der Rock

This skirt has four red buttons.

Dieser Rock hat vier rote Knöpfe.

sink¹ (kitchen) das Spülbecken, (bathroom) das Waschbecken

The sink is empty.

Das Waschbecken ist leer.

skate (on ice) Schlittschuh laufen, (on rollerskates) Rollschuh laufen

Gemma is skating.
Gemma läuft Schlittschuh.

sky — der Himmel

There's a plane in the sky.
Am Himmel ist ein Flugzeug.

sink² — unter/gehen*, sinken

Billy's boat is sinking.

Billys Boot sinkt.

ski — Ski fahren

Eric loves skiing.
Eric fährt sehr gern Ski.

sleep — schlafen

Hush! Adam is sleeping.
Pst! Adam schläft.

sit (be sitting) sitzen, (sit down) sich hin/setzen*

Sally is sitting on a blue stool.
Sally sitzt auf einem blauen Hocker.

Sit down!
Setz dich hin!

skin — die Haut, (fruit, vegetable) die Schale

smooth skin
weiche Haut

Banana skins aren't good to eat.
Bananenschalen sind nicht gut zum Essen.

sleeve — der Ärmel

Robert is wearing a yellow shirt with blue sleeves.

Robert trägt ein gelbes Hemd mit blauen Ärmeln.

a b c d e f g h i j k l m n o p q r s t u v w x y z

slice | die Scheibe, (cake) das Stück

a slice of bread
eine Scheibe Brot

a slice of cake
ein Stück Kuchen

slipper | der Hausschuh

Polly has pink, bunny-shaped slippers.

Polly hat rosa, häschenförmige Hausschuhe.

small | klein

Leila is a small girl.

Leila ist ein kleines Mädchen.

---

slide¹ | die Rutschbahn

There's a slide in the park.
Im Park ist eine Rutschbahn.

slow | langsam

This is an old, slow train.
Das hier ist ein alter, langsamer Zug.

smell | riechen

Smell the flowers!
Riech mal die Blumen!

This cat smells bad.
Diese Katze riecht schlecht.

---

slide² | rutschen

Denise is sliding down first.
Denise rutscht zuerst hinunter.

slowly | langsam

Sally is going slowly.
Sally fährt langsam.

smile | lächeln

Jack is smiling.
Jack lächelt.

---

slip | aus/rutschen*

Anna has slipped on the banana skin.

Anna ist auf der Bananenschale ausgerutscht.

slug | die Nacktschnecke

There are lots of slugs in the garden.

Im Garten sind viele Nacktschnecken.

smooth | glatt, (skin) weich

Babies have smooth skin.
Babys haben weiche Haut.

The road is smooth here.
Hier ist die Straße glatt.

---

a b c d e f g h i j k l m n o p q r **s** t u v w x y z

snail — die Schnecke

A snail has a shell on its back.

Eine Schnecke hat ein Haus auf ihrem Rücken.

snake — die Schlange

There's a snake in the tree.
Auf dem Baum ist eine Schlange.

snow — der Schnee, (to snow) schneien

They're playing in the snow.
Sie spielen im Schnee.

soap — die Seife

My soap is pink.
Meine Seife ist rosa.

soccer — der Fußball

Neil plays soccer every Saturday.
Neil spielt jeden Samstag Fußball.

sock — die Socke

Luke has striped socks.
Luke hat gestreifte Socken.

sofa — das Sofa

a comfortable sofa
ein bequemes Sofa

soft — weich

The kitten has soft, white fur.

Das Kätzchen hat ein weiches, weißes Fell.

soil — die Erde

My plant needs good soil.
Meine Pflanze braucht gute Erde.

soldier — der Soldat

Tony is dressed up as a soldier.
Tony ist als Soldat verkleidet.

song — das Lied

La la la la

Natalie is singing a song.
Natalie singt ein Lied.

soon — bald

It will soon be two o'clock.

Es ist bald zwei Uhr.

sort *to* spill

sort   **die Sorte, die Art**

different sorts of food
verschiedene Lebensmittelsorten

sound   **das Geräusch, der Ton**

Krächz!

That funny sound is just the parrot.
Das komische Geräusch ist bloß der Papagei.

soup   **die Suppe**

a can of vegetable soup

eine Dose
Gemüsesuppe

space   (place) **der Platz,** (outer space) **der Weltraum**

There are two free spaces.
Zwei Plätze sind frei.
There are billions of stars in space.
Im Weltraum sind Milliarden von Sternen.

spacecraft   **das Raumfahrzeug**

A rocket is a spacecraft.
Eine Rakete ist ein Raumfahrzeug.

speak   **sprechen**

Mrs. Rose is speaking to her friend.

Guten Tag! Wie geht's?

Frau Rose spricht mit ihrer Freundin.

special   **besonder-*, bestimmt**

a special day
ein besonderer Tag

Electricians need special tools.
Elektriker brauchen bestimmte Werkzeuge.

spell[1]   **der Zauberspruch**

The witch is casting a spell.
Die Hexe spricht einen Zauberspruch aus.

spell[2]   **buchstabieren, richtig schreiben können**

Oliver can spell his name.

OLIVER

Oliver kann seinen Namen richtig schreiben.

spend (money) **aus/geben**,** (time) **verbringen**

Danny spends his allowance on toys.
Danny gibt sein Taschengeld für Spielsachen aus.

spider   **die Spinne**

Maddy hates spiders, but I don't mind them.
Maddy kann Spinnen nicht leiden, aber mir machen sie nichts aus.

spill   **verschütten, aus/schütten**

The cat has spilled the mustard.

Die Katze hat den Senf ausgeschüttet.

a b c d e f g h i j k l m n o p q r **s** t u v w x y z

* You need to add an adjective ending to this word (see page 4).
** This is a separable verb (see page 99).

spinach — der Spinat

Spinach is a leafy vegetable.

Spinat
ist ein Blattgemüse.

splash — spritzen, verspritzen

Polly is splashing water everywhere.

Polly spritzt überall Wasser hin.

sponge — der Schwamm

a bath sponge
ein Badeschwamm

spoon — der Löffel

I need a spoon
to eat my soup.

Ich brauche
einen Löffel, um
meine Suppe zu essen.

sport — der Sport

They all enjoy playing sports.

Sie treiben alle gern Sport.

spot[1] — der Fleck, der Punkt

This dog has
black spots.
Dieser
Hund
hat
schwarze
Flecken.

a red skirt with yellow spots
ein roter Rock mit gelben Punkten

spot[2] — entdecken

I've spotted a clown.
Ich habe einen Clown entdeckt.

squirrel — das Eichhörnchen

a gray squirrel

ein
graues
Eichhörnchen

stairs — die Treppe

The stairs lead up
to the first floor.
Die Treppe
führt zum
ersten
Stock
hinauf.

stamp — die Briefmarke

This letter has a stamp on it.
Auf diesem Brief ist eine
Briefmarke.

Oliver Esser
Wurststraße 34
54321 Schokostadt

stand (be standing) stehen, (stand up) auf/stehen*

Alex is
standing.
Alex
steht.

Stand up,
please!
Steh bitte
auf!

star (in sky) der Stern, (person) der Star

The stars
are twinkling.
Die Sterne
funkeln.

Natalie, the
singer, is a big star.
Natalie, die Sängerin,
ist ein großer Star.

a b c d e f g h i j k l m n o p q r s t u v w x y z

start — an/fangen*

The birds are starting to eat the seeds.

Die Vögel fangen an, die Samen zu fressen.

station — der Bahnhof

There are two trains at the station.
Es sind zwei Züge im Bahnhof.

stay — (remain) bleiben, (visit) wohnen

The cows stay in the field.
Die Kühe bleiben auf der Weide.

He's staying at our house.
Er wohnt bei uns.

steep — steil

It's a steep path.
Es ist ein steiler Weg.

---

stick¹ — der Stock, (from a tree) der Zweig

a big stick
ein großer Zweig

a walking stick
ein Spazierstock

stick² — kleben

Polly is sticking her picture on the wall.
Polly klebt ihr Bild an die Wand.

still¹ — still

The car is standing still.
Das Auto steht still.

Milo is staying still.
Milo hält still.

still² — noch

Oliver's still hungry.
Oliver hat noch Hunger.

He still has some apples.
Er hat noch ein paar Äpfel.

---

sting — stechen

Bees can sting you.
Bienen können dich stechen.

stir — verrühren

Jack is stirring the mixture. — Jack verrührt die Mischung.

stone — der Stein

stones from the garden

Steine aus dem Garten

stool — der Hocker

a small, blue stool
ein kleiner, blauer Hocker

---

a b c d e f g h i j k l m n o p q r **s** t u v w x y z

stop *to* sugar

stop   an/halten*, (doing something) auf/hören*

Jan stops at the gate.
Jan hält an der Sperre an.

Stop that!
Hör auf damit!

---

storm   der Sturm

a storm at sea
ein Sturm auf See

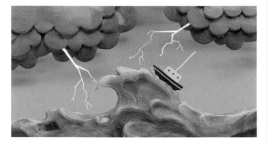

---

story   die Geschichte

Polly is writing a story.
Polly schreibt eine Geschichte.

Der Zauberring
von Polly Dot

Es war einmal eine schöne Prinzessin. Sie wohnte in einem prachtvollen Schloss mitten in einem Zauberwald. Eines Tages saß die Prinzessin im Garten.

---

straight   (line) gerade, (hair) glatt

a straight path
ein gerader Weg

Leslie has straight hair.
Leslie hat glatte Haare.

---

strawberry   die Erdbeere

a big, juicy strawberry

eine große, saftige Erdbeere

---

street   die Straße

a busy street
eine belebte Straße

---

string   der Bindfaden

Can you lend me some string?
Kannst du mir etwas Bindfaden leihen?

---

strong   stark, kräftig, (solid) stabil

a strong man
ein kräftiger Mann

The stool isn't very strong.
Der Hocker ist nicht sehr stabil.

strong coffee
starker Kaffee

---

study¹   das Arbeitszimmer

Mom's study   Muttis Arbeitszimmer

---

study²   lernen, (a topic) sich befassen mit

Sara is studying hard.
Sara lernt fleißig.

She is studying the Romans.
Sie befasst sich mit den Römern.

---

suddenly   plötzlich, auf einmal

Suddenly I feel sick.
Mir ist plötzlich schlecht.

Suddenly Asha drops the vase.
Auf einmal lässt Asha die Vase fallen.

---

sugar   der Zucker

I need sugar to make a cake.
Ich brauche Zucker, um einen Kuchen zu machen.

---

a b c d e f g h i j k l m n o p q r s t u v w x y z

suitcase — der Koffer

This is Mr. Brand's suitcase.
Das ist Herr Brands Koffer.

sunglasses — die Sonnenbrille

Polly has pink sunglasses with blue flowers.

Polly hat eine rosa Sonnenbrille mit blauen Blumen darauf.

swan — der Schwan

There's a swan on the river.

Auf dem Fluss ist ein Schwan.

sum — die Rechenaufgabe, die Summe

These sums are easy.
Diese Rechenaufgaben sind leicht.

$$8 + 2 =$$
$$4 - 2 =$$
$$10 \times 4 =$$

supermarket — der Supermarkt

Dad is at the supermarket.

Vati ist im Supermarkt.

sweep — fegen, kehren

Anna is sweeping the path.
Anna fegt den Weg.

Shall I sweep the floor?
Soll ich kehren?

sun — die Sonne

The sun is shining.
Die Sonne scheint.

sure — sicher

Dad says, "Have we got everything? Are you sure?"
Vati sagt: „Haben wir alles? Bist du sicher?"

sweet — (taste) süß, (cute) niedlich, süß

That's a very sweet kitten.
Das ist ein sehr niedliches Kätzchen.

The cake is very sweet.
Der Kuchen ist sehr süß.

sunflower — die Sonnenblume

Aggie has some lovely sunflowers.

Aggie hat ein paar schöne Sonnenblumen.

surprise — die Überraschung

What a surprise!
Was für eine Überraschung!

BUH!

swim — schwimmen

Pete can swim very well.
Pete kann sehr gut schwimmen.

a b c d e f g h i j k l m n o p q r **s** t u v w x y z

swimming pool das Schwimmbad

We're going to the swimming pool today.

Wir gehen heute ins Schwimmbad.

swimsuit der Badeanzug

Minnie is wearing a striped swimsuit.
Minnie hat einen gestreiften Badeanzug an.

swing¹ die Schaukel

There are swings in the park.
Im Park sind Schaukeln.

swing² schaukeln

The girls are swinging.
Die Mädchen schaukeln.

table der Tisch

a wooden table
ein Holztisch

tail der Schwanz

This dog has a long tail.
Dieser Hund hat einen langen Schwanz.

take nehmen, mit/nehmen*, (away) weg/nehmen*

Amy's taking sand in her wagon.
Amy nimmt Sand in ihrem Anhänger mit.

Someone's taken my flowers.
Jemand hat mir meine Blumen weggenommen.

talk sprechen, sich unterhalten

The ladies are talking.

Die Damen unterhalten sich.

tall (person, animal) groß, (building) hoch, hoh-**

A giraffe is a very tall animal.
Eine Giraffe ist ein sehr großes Tier.

a tall skyscraper
ein hoher Wolkenkratzer

taste schmecken, (take a little) probieren

Ethan is tasting his ice cream.
Ethan probiert sein Eis.

It tastes good.
Es schmeckt gut.

taxi das Taxi

a yellow taxi
ein gelbes Taxi

tea der Tee

a tea bag
ein Teebeutel

a b c d e f g h i j k l m n o p q r s t u v w x y z

* This is a separable verb (see page 99).
** You need to add an adjective ending to this word (see page 4).

teacher *to* thirsty

teacher	**der Lehrer die Lehrerin**

Our teacher is Mr. Levy.

Unser Lehrer heißt Herr Levy.

---

team   **die Mannschaft**

This is Neil's team.
Das hier ist Neils Mannschaft.

---

teddy bear   **der Teddy**

This teddy bear has a red scarf.

Dieser Teddy hat einen roten Schal.

---

telephone   **das Telefon**

Where is the telephone, please?
Wo ist das Telefon, bitte?

---

television   **das Fernsehen, (television set) der Fernseher**

There's nothing on television this evening.
Heute Abend kommt nichts im Fernsehen.

a new television
ein neuer Fernseher

---

tell   **sagen, (a story) erzählen**

Mrs. Beef is telling them the story.
Frau Beef erzählt ihnen die Geschichte.

Tell me what you think.
Sag mir, was du meinst.

---

tent   **das Zelt**

Jack has a little, yellow tent.
Jack hat ein kleines, gelbes Zelt.

---

thank   **danken, sich bedanken**

Polly is thanking Marco for her present.
Polly dankt Marco für ihr Geschenk *or* Polly bedankt sich bei Marco für ihr Geschenk.

Danke sehr!

---

thin   **dünn**

thin string
dünner Bindfaden

a thin cat
eine dünne Katze

---

thing   **die Sache, das Ding**

Tina still has some things to do.

Tina hat noch einige Sachen zu erledigen.

What's that thing?
Was ist das Ding da?

---

think   **(believe) glauben, denken, (consider) meinen, finden**

I think he is ready.
Ich glaube, er ist fertig.
Maddy thinks spiders are horrible.
What do you think?
Maddy findet Spinnen scheußlich.
Was meinst du?

(to be) thirsty   **Durst haben**

Polly is very thirsty.
Polly hat großen Durst.

---

a b c d e f g h i j k l m n o p q r s **t** u v w x y z

through   durch

Mr. Bun is going out through the front door.
Herr Bun geht durch die Haustür hinaus.

throw   werfen, (to someone) zu/werfen*

Anna is throwing the ball to Jack.
Anna wirft Jack den Ball zu.

Don't throw stones!
Wirf keine Steine!

thumb   der Daumen

This is Polly's thumb.
Das hier ist Pollys Daumen.

ticket   die Karte, (train, bus) die Fahrkarte

I've bought my ticket.
Ich habe meine Fahrkarte gekauft.

tie   binden

Someone has tied the ribbons.
Jemand hat die Bänder gebunden.

tiger   der Tiger

Tigers live in Asia.
Tiger leben in Asien.

time   (on a clock) Uhr, (time taken) die Zeit

What time is it?
Wie viel Uhr ist es?

I don't have much time.
Ich habe nicht viel Zeit.

tiny   winzig

a small cat and a tiny cat

eine kleine Katze und eine winzige Katze

tip   die Spitze, das Ende

The tip of this fox's tail is white.

Dieser Fuchsschwanz hat ein weißes Ende.

the tip of the pencil die Bleistiftspitze

toast   der Toast

The toast is ready.
Der Toast ist fertig.

toddler   das Kleinkind

Joshua is still a toddler.
Joshua ist noch ein Kleinkind.

toe   die Zehe

Your toes are at the end of your feet.
Die Zehen sind am Ende der Füße.

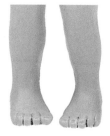

a b c d e f g h i j k l m n o p q r s t u v w x y z

together — zusammen

Jenny and Ethan are playing together.

Jenny und Ethan spielen zusammen.

tonight — heute Abend,
(in the night) **heute Nacht**

Ich gehe heute Abend ins Theater.

She's going to the theatre tonight.

(on) top — oben

The kitten is on top of the desk.

Das Kätzchen sitzt oben auf dem Schreibtisch.

toilet — die Toilette

a blue toilet
eine blaue Toilette

tooth — der Zahn

Zach is showing his teeth.
Zach zeigt seine Zähne.

touch — berühren

The label says "Do not touch."

I can touch my toes.
Ich kann meine Zehen berühren.

Nicht berühren

tomato — die Tomate

a nice, ripe tomato
eine schöne, reife Tomate

toothbrush — die Zahnbürste

This is Zach's toothbrush.

Das hier ist Zachs Zahnbürste.

towel — das Handtuch,
(bath, beach) **das Badetuch**

Anna has a big, blue towel.
Anna hat ein großes, blaues Badetuch.

tongue — die Zunge

Luke is sticking his tongue out.
Luke streckt die Zunge heraus.

toothpaste — die Zahnpasta

mint flavor toothpaste

Zahnpasta mit Pfefferminzgeschmack

town — die Stadt

This is the town center.
Das ist die Stadtmitte.

a b c d e f g h i j k l m n o p q r s t u v w x y z

toy *to* twin

toy — das Spielzeug, (toys) die Spielsachen

Joshua has lots of toys.

Joshua hat viele Spielsachen.

tractor — der Traktor

The farmer has a red tractor.
Der Bauer hat einen roten Traktor.

train — der Zug

an express train
ein Schnellzug

tree — der Baum

There are lots of trees in the park.

Im Park sind viele Bäume.

truck — der Lastwagen

a big, green truck
ein großer, grüner Lastwagen

Lehmanns Lastwagen

true — wahr, richtig

RICHTIG ODER FALSCH?
A. Ein Ozelot ist eine Pflanzenart.
B. Pinguine können nicht fliegen.

True or false?

It's a true story.
Es ist eine wahre Geschichte.

try — versuchen, (take a little) probieren

They are trying to move the package.
Sie versuchen, das Paket umzustellen.

Can I try your ice cream?
Kann ich dein Eis probieren?

T-shirt — das T-Shirt

Ash is wearing a red and yellow T-shirt.
Ash trägt ein rotgelbes T-Shirt.

turkey — der Truthahn

A turkey is an American bird.

Der Truthahn ist ein amerikanischer Vogel.

turn — ab/biegen*, sich drehen

Jan's turning left.
Jan biegt links ab.

The wheels are turning.
Die Räder drehen sich.

TV — das Fernsehen, (TV set) der Fernseher

What's on TV this evening?
Was kommt heute Abend im Fernsehen?

a new TV
ein neuer Fernseher

twin — der Zwilling

Bill and Ben are twins.
Bill und Ben sind Zwillinge.

a b c d e f g h i j k l m n o p q r s t u v w x y z

* This is a separable verb (see page 99).

Uu ugly *to* usually

ugly — hässlich

This fish is ugly.
Dieser Fisch ist hässlich.

umbrella — der Regenschirm

Robert has a big umbrella.

Robert hat einen großen Regenschirm.

under — unter

The kitten is hiding under the boards.

Das Kätzchen hält sich unter den Brettern versteckt.

understand — verstehen

I don't understand what Ben is saying.
Ich verstehe nicht, was Ben sagt.

Bäh bäh öh!

undress — aus/ziehen*, (yourself) sich aus/ziehen*

Luke is undressing.
Luke zieht sich aus.

unhappy — unglücklich

Liddy feels very unhappy.

Liddy ist sehr unglücklich.

upright — (person) gerade, (wall, pillar) senkrecht

Tony is standing upright.
Tony hält sich gerade.

The goalposts aren't upright.
Die Torpfosten sind nicht senkrecht.

upset — (worried) aufgeregt, (sad) betrübt, bestürzt

Mrs. Beef is upset.
Frau Beef ist aufgeregt.

upside down — verkehrt herum

The picture is upside down.

Das Bild hängt verkehrt herum.

use — benutzen

Mr. Clack is using a saw.
Herr Clack benutzt eine Säge.

useful — nützlich

A wheelbarrow is very useful in the garden.
Eine Schubkarre ist im Garten sehr nützlich.

usually — gewöhnlich, normalerweise

Sara usually cycles to school.
Sara fährt gewöhnlich mit dem Rad zur Schule.

a b c d e f g h i j k l m n o p q r s t **u** v w x y z

* This is a separable verb (see page 99).

Vv vacuum cleaner *to* voice

Ww wait *to* wake

vacuum cleaner — der Staubsauger

Where's the vacuum cleaner?

Wo ist der Staubsauger?

view — die Aussicht, der Blick

a nice view of the country

ein schöner Blick auf die Landschaft

wait — warten

They are waiting for the bus.
Sie warten auf den Bus.

vase — die Vase

a vase with purple flowers in it

eine Vase mit violetten Blumen darin

visit — (person) besuchen, (place) besichtigen

The children are visiting the museum.
Die Kinder besichtigen das Museum.

waiter — der Kellner

The waiter is bringing a cup of tea.
Der Kellner bringt eine Tasse Tee.

vegetable — das Gemüse

different vegetables

verschiedene Gemüsesorten

visitor — der Gast

The visitors are arriving.
Die Gäste kommen an.

waitress — die Kellnerin

The waitress is bringing two cups of coffee.

Die Kellnerin bringt zwei Tassen Kaffee.

very — sehr

Flora is dirty and Sally is very dirty.
Flora ist schmutzig und Sally ist sehr schmutzig.

voice — die Stimme

Molly has a lovely voice.

Laaaaaa!

Molly hat eine schöne Stimme.

wake — (someone) wecken, (wake up) auf/wachen*

Sam is waking up.
Sam wacht auf.

a b c d e f g h i j k l m n o p q r s t u v w x y z

* This is a separable verb (see page 99).

85

walk **laufen,**
(go on foot) **zu Fuß gehen**

Danny is
walking fast.
**Danny läuft
schnell.**

He walks
to school.
**Er geht zu
Fuß zur
Schule.**

wall (outside) **die Mauer,**
(inside) **die Wand**

The hens
are sitting on
a stone wall.
**Die Hühner
sitzen auf einer
Steinmauer.**

want **wollen**

Jenny wants some more wagons.

**Jenny will noch ein paar
Waggons.**

warm **warm**

Renata is wearing a
nice, warm coat.
**Renata hat einen
schönen, warmen
Mantel an.**

wash **waschen,**
(yourself) **sich waschen**

Jack is
washing.
**Jack
wäscht
sich.**

washing machine

die Waschmaschine

a new
washing
machine
**eine neue
Waschmaschine**

watch¹ **die Uhr,**
die Armbanduhr

Polly got a new
watch for her
birthday.

Polly
hat zum
Geburtstag eine
neue Uhr bekommen.

watch² **an/schauen*,**
an/sehen*

They are all watching
the clown.

Sie schauen alle den Clown an
or **Sie sehen alle den Clown an.**

water **das Wasser**

Becky is playing
in the water.
**Becky spielt
im Wasser.**

wave¹ **die Welle**

a big wave **eine große Welle**

wave² **winken,**
(to someone) **zu/winken***

Polly is waving to her friends.
**Polly
winkt
ihren
Freunden
zu.**

way (route) **der Weg,**
(method) **die Art**

a good way to cook eggs
**eine gute Art, Eier
zu kochen**

the way to
the village
**der Weg
zum Dorf**

a b c d e f g h i j k l m n o p q r s t u v w x y z

* This is a separable verb (see page 99).

wear — tragen, an/haben*

Miriam is wearing a red suit.
Miriam trägt ein rotes Kostüm *or* **Miriam hat ein rotes Kostüm an.**

weather — das Wetter

What's the weather like today?
Wie ist das Wetter heute?

web — (spider's) das Netz, World Wide Web das Internet

a spider's web
ein Spinnennetz

I'm searching the Web.
Ich suche im Internet.
a website
eine Internetseite *or* **eine Website**

week — die Woche

There are seven days in a week.
Die Woche hat sieben Tage.

Montag
Dienstag
Mittwoch
Donnerstag
Freitag
Samstag
Sonntag

well — gut

How are you? Very well, thank you.
Wie geht's? Danke, sehr gut.

Sara reads very well.
Sara liest sehr gut.

wet — nass

Jem the plumber is all wet.
Klempner Jem ist ganz nass.

whale — der Wal

This whale can swim very fast.

Dieser Wal kann sehr schnell schwimmen.

wheel — das Rad

a big truck wheel

ein großes Lastwagenrad

while — während

Jack is eating cake while his parents are talking.
Jack isst Kuchen, während seine Eltern sich unterhalten.

wide — breit, weit

The sofa is quite wide.

Das Sofa ist ziemlich breit.
a wide skirt
ein weiter Rock

wild — wild

These are all wild animals.

Dies sind alle wilde Tiere.

win — gewinnen

The pink cake has won first prize.
Der rosa Kuchen hat den ersten Preis gewonnen.

wind   der Wind

The wind is blowing.
Der Wind weht.

---

window   das Fenster

Look out of the window.
Schau zum Fenster hinaus!

---

wish   der Wunsch, (make a wish) sich etwas wünschen

The fairy can grant three wishes.
Die Fee kann drei Wünsche erfüllen.

Did you make a wish?
Hast du dir etwas gewünscht?

---

witch   die Hexe

There are often witches in fairy tales.
In Märchen kommen oft Hexen vor.

---

with   mit

Ben sleeps with his teddy bear.
Ben schläft mit seinem Teddy.

a bird with blue feet
ein Vogel mit blauen Füßen

---

woman   die Frau

This woman is a gardener.
Diese Frau ist Gärtnerin.

---

wood   das Holz, (trees) der Wald

This table is made of wood.
Dieser Tisch ist aus Holz.

There are woods beside the lake.
Neben dem See liegt ein Wald.

---

word   das Wort

a list of words
eine Liste mit Wörtern

Adresse
brennen
Drache
leer

---

work   (do a job) arbeiten, (function) funktionieren

Mick works all day.
Mick arbeitet den ganzen Tag.

This computer doesn't work.
Dieser Computer funktioniert nicht.

---

world   die Welt

Mr. Brand is traveling around the world.

Herr Brand macht eine Weltreise.

---

write   schreiben

Oliver is writing his name.
Oliver schreibt seinen Namen.

OLIVER

---

wrong   (incorrect) falsch, (bad) unrecht

the wrong answers
die falschen Antworten

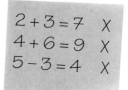

$2 + 3 = 7$ X
$4 + 6 = 9$ X
$5 - 3 = 4$ X

It's wrong to steal.
Es ist unrecht zu stehlen.

Xx x *to* xylophone

x — das Kreuz, (in math) x

Put an "x" in the box.
Mach ein Kreuz in das Kästchen.

$$2 \times 2 = 4$$

(two times two equals four)
(zwei mal zwei ist vier)

Xmas — Weihnachten

Merry Xmas!

Frohe Weihnachten!

---

x-ray — das Röntgenbild, (have an x-ray) geröntgt werden

The x-ray shows Robert's skeleton.
Das Röntgenbild zeigt Roberts Skelett.

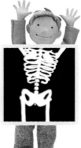

Robert is having an x-ray.
Robert wird geröntgt.

---

xylophone — das Xylophon

This xylophone has six notes.
Dieses Xylophon hat sechs Töne.

Yy yawn *to* young

yawn — gähnen

Sam's yawning.
Sam gähnt.

---

year — das Jahr

Flora is five years old. Annie is a year older.
Flora ist fünf Jahre alt. Annie ist ein Jahr älter.

---

yet — noch

Ben can't walk yet.
Ben kann noch nicht laufen.

---

young — jung, (children) klein

young people
junge Leute

young children
kleine Kinder

Zz zebra *to* zoo [z]

zebra — das Zebra

Zebras live in Africa.
Zebras leben in Afrika.

---

zero — null

Five take away five equals zero.
Fünf weniger fünf ist null.

$$5 - 5 = 0$$

---

zipper — der Reißverschluss

The zipper is half open.
Der Reißverschluss ist halb offen.

---

zoo — der Zoo, der Tiergarten

There's a panda at the zoo.
Im Zoo ist ein Panda.

a b c d e f g h i j k l m n o p q r s t u v w x y z

Colors

Farben

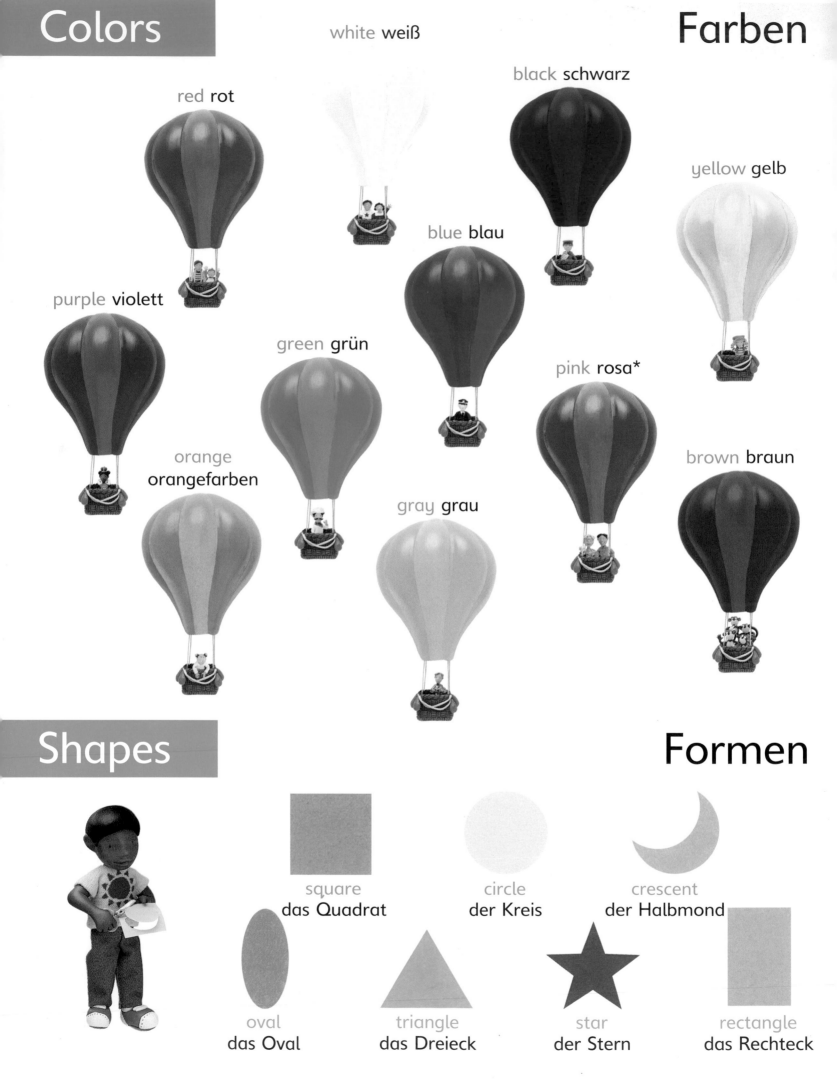

white weiß

red rot

black schwarz

blue blau

yellow gelb

purple violett

green grün

pink rosa*

orange
orangefarben

gray grau

brown braun

Shapes

Formen

square
das Quadrat

circle
der Kreis

crescent
der Halbmond

oval
das Oval

triangle
das Dreieck

star
der Stern

rectangle
das Rechteck

* This word is always spelled the same. You don't need to add on any adjective endings.

Numbers

Zahlen

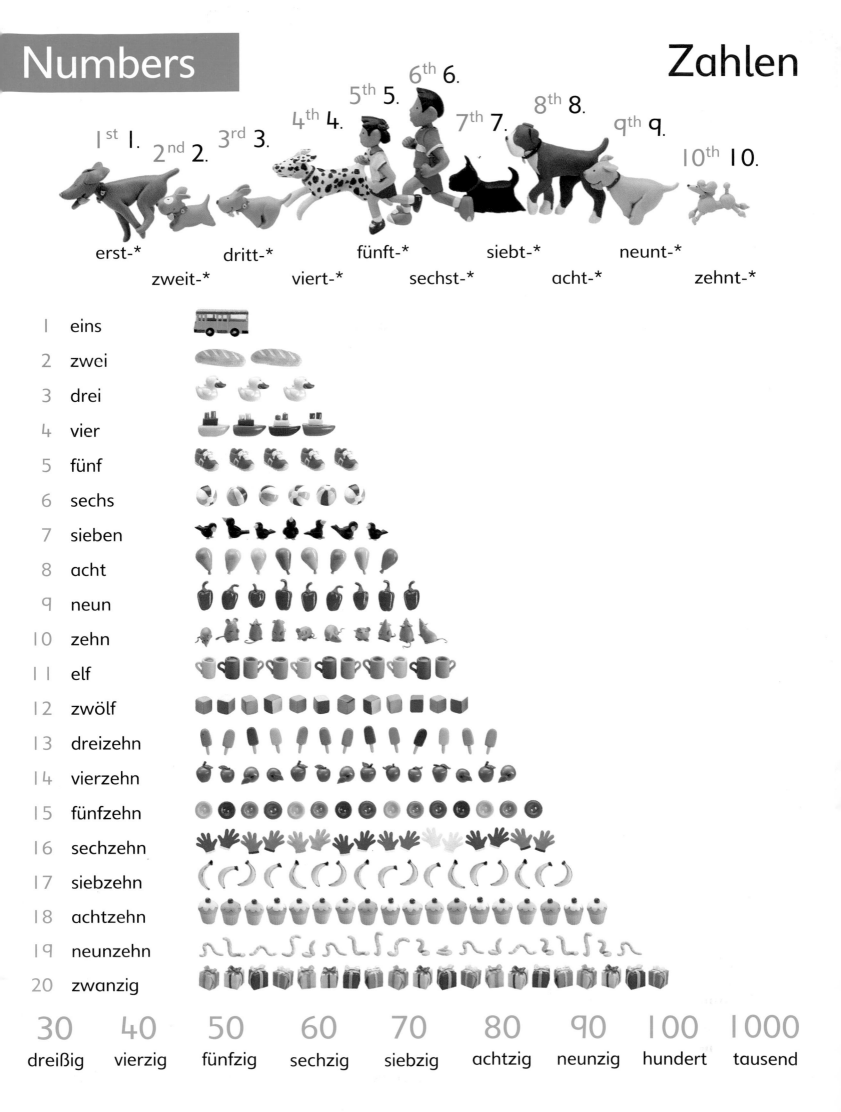

1st 1.   2nd 2.   3rd 3.   4th 4.   5th 5.   6th 6.   7th 7.   8th 8.   9th 9.   10th 10.

erst-*   zweit-*   dritt-*   viert-*   fünft-*   sechst-*   siebt-*   acht-*   neunt-*   zehnt-*

1	eins
2	zwei
3	drei
4	vier
5	fünf
6	sechs
7	sieben
8	acht
9	neun
10	zehn
11	elf
12	zwölf
13	dreizehn
14	vierzehn
15	fünfzehn
16	sechzehn
17	siebzehn
18	achtzehn
19	neunzehn
20	zwanzig

30	40	50	60	70	80	90	100	1000
dreißig	vierzig	fünfzig	sechzig	siebzig	achtzig	neunzig	hundert	tausend

* You need to add an adjective ending to these words (see page 4): my first day at school – mein erster Schultag.

Days and months

Die Tage und Monate

Monday
Montag

Tuesday
Dienstag

Wednesday
Mittwoch

Thursday
Donnerstag

Friday
Freitag

Saturday
Samstag

Sunday
Sonntag

January Januar

February Februar

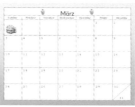
March März

April April

May Mai

June Juni

July Juli

August August

September September

October Oktober

November November

December Dezember

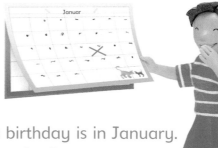

Polly's birthday is in January.
Polly hat im Januar
Geburtstag.

92

Die Jahreszeiten

Spring **der Frühling**

Summer **der Sommer**

Fall **der Herbst**

Winter **der Winter**

Family

Die Familie

Polly's photo album
Pollys Fotoalbum

sister, brother
die Schwester, der Bruder

father	mother
der Vater	**die Mutter**
Dad	Mom
Vati	**Mutti**

son
der Sohn

daughter
die Tochter

grandmother		grandfather
die Großmutter		**der Großvater**
Granny	grandchildren	Grandpa
Oma	**die Enkelkinder**	**Opa**

Dad and his brother
Vati und sein Bruder

baby
das Baby

grandparents		parents
die Großeltern		**die Eltern**
	children	
	die Kinder	

aunt (girl) cousin
die Tante die Cousine*
uncle
der Onkel

* boy cousin would be *der Cousin.*

94

Words we use a lot

On these pages you'll find some words that are useful for making sentences. Remember that in German some words can change their spelling, depending on whether the word that follows is masculine, feminine, neuter or plural, and on what part the word plays in a sentence (see page 4).

about	(story) über, (roughly) ungefähr	in, into	in	they	sie
across	über	it	er (sie, es)	through	durch
again	wieder *or* noch einmal	maybe	vielleicht	to	zu, (a town *or* country) nach, (in order to) um . . . zu
almost	fast	me	mich, (to *or* for me) mir	today	heute
also	auch			tomorrow	morgen
always	immer	never	nie	too	(also) auch, (too much, too hot) zu
and	und	no	(not yes) nein, (not one) kein (keine, kein, keine)		
another	noch ein (eine, ein)			under	unter
at	(a place) an *or* bei (a time) um	no one	niemand	until	bis
		nothing	nichts	us	uns
because	weil	nowhere	nirgends		
but	aber			we	wir
by	(beside) neben, (done by) von, (by car, bus) mit	often	oft	what	was
		on	(something flat) auf, (something vertical) an	where	wo
				with	mit
		or	oder	without	ohne
each *or* every	jeder (jede, jedes)	she	sie	yes	ja
everybody *or* everyone	alle *or* jeder	since	(time) seit, (because) da	yesterday	gestern
everything	alles	so	(so big) so, (because of this) also	you	du, ihr *or* Sie*, (to *or* for you) dir, euch *or* Ihnen
everywhere	überall	some	(of one thing) etwas, (several things) ein paar *or* einige		
for	für	somebody *or* someone	jemand		
from	von	something	etwas		
		sometimes	manchmal		
he	er	somewhere	irgendwo		
her	sie, (to *or* for her) ihr, (belonging to her) ihr (ihre, ihr, ihre)	them	sie, (to *or* for them) ihnen		
here	hier, (to here) hierher	then	(next) dann, (at that time) damals		
him	ihn, (to *or* for him) ihm	there	da *or* dort, (to there) dahin *or* dorthin		
I	ich				
if	wenn				

* For the difference between *du, ihr* and *Sie*, see page 4.

95

This, that

On page 3, you can see how the word for "the" changes, depending on whether a noun is masculine, feminine or neuter. The word for "this" is *dieser* and it changes in a similar way:

the boy	der Junge
this boy	dieser Junge
the woman	die Frau
this woman	diese Frau
the house	das Haus
this house	dieses Haus

When you are talking about more than one of something (plurals), the word for "these" is *diese* for masculine, feminine and neuter nouns:

these boys	diese Jungen
these women	diese Frauen
these houses	diese Häuser

Sometimes you will see different endings. This is because the endings change depending on what part "this thing" or "these things" are playing in a sentence:

This apple tastes good.
Dieser Apfel schmeckt gut.

Do you want this apple?
Willst du diesen Apfel?

The German word for "that" is *jener*. It changes in a similar way to *dieser*.

that boy	jener Junge
that woman	jene Frau
that house	jenes Haus

The word for "those" is *jene*:

those boys	jene Jungen
those women	jene Frauen
those houses	jene Häuser

My, your, his, her

In German, the words for "my," "your," "his," "her," "our" and "their" change slightly, depending on whether the noun that follows is masculine, feminine, neuter or plural. The word for "my" is *mein*. Here's how it changes:

my brother	mein Bruder
my mother	meine Mutter
my house	mein Haus
my parents	meine Eltern

If you're talking to a younger person or someone you know very well, the word for "your" is *dein*. If you're talking to two or more people you know very well, it's *euer*. And if you're talking to one or more people you don't know so well, it's *Ihr*.

your brother
dein Bruder, euer Bruder *or* Ihr Bruder
your mother
deine Mutter, eure Mutter *or* Ihre Mutter
your house
dein Haus, euer Haus *or* Ihr Haus
your parents
deine Eltern, eure Eltern *or* Ihre Eltern

The word for "his" is *sein*:

his brother	sein Bruder
his mother	seine Mutter
his house	sein Haus
his parents	seine Eltern

The word for "her" and "their" is *ihr*. And the word for "our" is *unser*.

her brother *or* their brother	ihr Bruder
her mother *or* their mother	ihre Mutter
our house	unser Haus
our parents	unsere Eltern

Making sentences

To make sentences in German, you often put the words in the same order as in an English sentence:

The baker sells fresh bread.
Der Bäcker verkauft frisches Brot.

The bus is going into town.
Der Bus fährt in die Stadt.

But German word order is sometimes very different from English. In German, the verb (or "doing" word) is usually the second idea in the sentence. So, if you start a sentence with a word or phrase such as "today" or "in the summer," the verb must come next:

Today we're going to the park.
Heute gehen wir in den Park.

In the summer I play tennis.
Im Sommer spiele ich Tennis.

Sometimes, you have to put the verb at the end of a sentence, for example, after the words *wenn* ("if" or "when"), *weil* ("because"), *während* ("while"), *bis* ("until") and *da* ("since"):

I wear gloves when it's cold.
Ich trage Handschuhe, wenn es kalt ist.

Liddy is sad because she misses her mom.
Liddy ist traurig, weil sie ihre Mutti vermisst.

Often, a sentence has two verbs, with the second one in the infinitive (the "to" form): "I want to go home." In German, the second verb goes to the end of the sentence:

I want to play soccer.
Ich will Fußball spielen.

I have to do my homework.
Ich muss meine Hausaufgaben machen.

Can I have some more strawberries?
Kann ich noch Erdbeeren haben?

More and most

In English, when you compare things, you often add "er" to an adjective: "A mouse is smaller than a rabbit." Other times, you use "more": "My puzzle is more difficult than yours." In German, you always add *-er* to the adjective:

Cars are faster than bicycles.
Autos sind schneller als Fahrräder.

With some short adjectives, you need to add an umlaut (¨) as well:

Olivia is taller than Joshua.
Olivia ist größer als Joshua.

Joshua is older than Ben.
Joshua ist älter als Ben.

When you compare several things, in English you usually add "est" to the adjective or use "most": "the tallest tree" or "the most delicious cake." In German, you add *-ste* to the adjective:

the fastest car
das schnellste Auto

Again, with some short adjectives, you need to add an umlaut (¨):

the longest river
der längste Fluss

the youngest baby
das jüngste Baby

As in English, there are special words for:

better   besser
the best   der, die *or* das beste

My plane is better than your car.
Mein Flugzeug ist besser als dein Auto.

the best pupil
der beste Schüler *or* die beste Schülerin

Making questions

To make a question in German, you put the verb before the subject of the sentence and add a question mark:

Is the bus going into town?
Fährt der Bus in die Stadt?

Is the kitten behind the flowerpot?
Ist das Kätzchen hinter dem Blumentopf?

You can also make questions beginning with question words, such as:

Who..?	Wer..?
Which..?	Welcher..?, Welche..?, Welches..? *or* Welche..?
What..?	Was..?
Where..?	Wo..?
When..?	Wann..?
Why..?	Warum..?
How..? *or* What...like?	Wie..?
How much..?	Wie viel..?
How many..?	Wie viele..?

For example:

How many CDs do you have?
Wie viele CDs hast du?

What's the weather like today?
Wie ist das Wetter heute?

And there are some other useful words for questions, which begin with "any–" in English:

anybody *or* anyone	jemand
anything	etwas
anywhere	irgendwo

For example:

Is anybody in the classroom?
Ist jemand im Klassenzimmer?

Do you need anything?
Brauchst du etwas?

Have you seen my glasses anywhere?
Hast du irgendwo meine Brille gesehen?

Negative sentences

A negative sentence is a "not" sentence, such as "I'm not tired." To make a sentence negative in German, you add the word *nicht*:

I'm not tired.
Ich bin nicht müde.

This bus isn't going into town.
Dieser Bus fährt nicht in die Stadt.

The kitten isn't under the table.
Das Kätzchen ist nicht unter dem Tisch.

To say "no . . .", "not a . . ." or "not any . . .", you use *kein* with masculine nouns, *keine* with feminine nouns, *kein* with neuter nouns and *keine* with plural nouns. For example:

That's not a dog.
Das ist kein Hund.

She's not wearing a cap.
Sie trägt keine Mütze.

We don't eat meat *or* We eat no meat.
Wir essen kein Fleisch.

I have no pets *or* I don't have any pets.
Ich habe keine Haustiere.

Here are some more useful words for negative sentences:

nobody *or* no one	niemand
nothing	nichts
never	nie

This is how they're used:

There is nobody at home
  or There isn't anybody at home.
Niemand ist zu Hause.

I have nothing to eat
  or I don't have anything to eat.
Ich habe nichts zu essen.

The train is never late
  or The train isn't ever late.
Der Zug kommt nie zu spät.

Verbs

The next few pages list the verbs (or "doing" words) that appear in the main part of the dictionary. Page 4 explains a little about verbs in German, and how the endings change for "I," "you," "he," "she," and so on.

To use a verb in the present (the form you use to talk about things that are happening now), you start with the infinitive (the "to" form) and take off the -en. Then you add these endings:

ich - I	-e
du - you (singular)	-st
er, sie, es - he, she, it	-t
wir - we	-en
ihr - you (plural)	-t
sie - they	-en
Sie - you (polite)	-en

For example, the verb "to do" is *machen*. To say "I do," you take off the -en and add -e (*ich mache*). To say "he does," you add -t (*er macht*), and so on. On the following pages, you'll find the infinitive (the "to" form) and the "he, she *or* it" form of each verb.

Some verbs change their spelling slightly in the "you" (*du*) form and in the "he, she *or* it" form. These verbs are listed with the "I" form as well, so you can see how the spelling changes:

to speak	sprechen
I speak	ich spreche
he speaks	er spricht

A few verbs, such as the verbs *sein* ("to be") and *haben* ("to have"), don't follow the normal pattern. These verbs are listed in full.

Reflexive verbs

Reflexive verbs are a special kind of verb. They are often used where in English you would use ". . . myself," ". . . yourself," and so on. The main part of the verb works just like other verbs, but you need to add an extra word depending on who is doing the action. For example, *sich waschen* ("to wash yourself") is formed like this:

I wash myself	ich wasche mich
you wash yourself	du wäschst dich
he washes himself, she washes herself *or* it washes itself	er, sie *or* es wäscht sich
we wash ourselves	wir waschen uns
you wash yourselves	ihr wascht euch
they wash themselves	sie waschen sich
you wash yourself *or* you wash yourselves	Sie waschen sich

Separable verbs

Some German verbs, called separable verbs, split up when you use them in a sentence. For example, the verb "to open" is *aufmachen*, but when you use it in a sentence it looks like this:

She opens the door.
Sie macht die Tür auf.

Please open the window!
Mach bitte das Fenster auf!

In the main part of the dictionary and in the verb list on the following pages, separable verbs are shown like this: *auf/machen*. The slash shows you where the verb splits.

Verbs

ab/biegen — to turn
er biegt ab (left, right)

ab/lecken — to lick (of
er leckt ab animals)

ab/schreiben — to copy
er schreibt ab (writing)

sich ab/trocknen — to
er trocknet dry
  sich ab yourself

sich amüsieren — to
er amüsiert enjoy
  sich yourself

an/fangen — to start
ich fange an
er fängt an

angeln — to fish
ich angle
er angelt

an/haben* — to wear
ich habe an
er hat an

an/halten — to stop
ich halte an
er hält an

an/kommen — to arrive
er kommt an

an/schauen to look (at),
er schaut an to watch

an/sehen to look (at),
ich sehe an to watch
er sieht an

antworten to answer,
er antwortet to reply

an/ziehen — to dress
er zieht an (someone)

sich an/ziehen to dress
er zieht (yourself)
  sich an

arbeiten — to work
er arbeitet

atmen to breathe
er atmet

auf/bewahren to keep
er bewahrt auf (store)

auf/hören — to stop
er hört auf

auf/machen — to open
er macht auf

auf/stehen to stand up
er steht auf

auf/wachen to wake up
er wacht auf

auf/wärmen to heat
er wärmt auf (food)

aus/geben to spend
ich gebe aus (money)
er gibt aus

aus/rutschen to slip
er rutscht aus

aus/schneiden to cut
er schneidet aus out

aus/schütten to spill
er schüttet aus

aus/suchen to choose,
er sucht aus to pick

aus/ziehen to
er zieht aus undress
(someone)

sich aus/ziehen to
er zieht undress
  sich aus (yourself)

backen to bake
ich backe
er backt or er bäckt

balancieren to balance
er balanciert

bauen to build
er baut

sich bedanken to thank
er bedankt sich

bedeuten to mean
er bedeutet

sich beeilen to hurry,
er beeilt sich to rush

sich befassen mit to
er befasst study
  sich mit (a topic)

befühlen to feel
er befühlt (touch)

begegnen to meet
er begegnet (by chance)

beginnen to begin
er beginnt

behalten to keep
ich behalte
er behält

beißen to bite
er beißt

bellen to bark
er bellt

bemerken to notice
er bemerkt

benutzen to use
er benutzt

berühren to touch
er berührt

besichtigen to visit
er besichtigt (a place)

besuchen to visit
er besucht (a person)

sich bewegen to move
er bewegt (yourself)
  sich

bezahlen to pay for
er bezahlt

binden to tie
er bindet

blasen to blow
ich blase
er bläst

bleiben to stay
er bleibt (remain)

braten to fry
ich brate
er brät

brauchen to need
er braucht

brechen to break
ich breche
er bricht

brennen to burn
er brennt

bringen to bring
er bringt

buchstabieren to spell
er buchstabiert

bügeln to iron
er bügelt

danken to thank
er dankt

denken to think
er denkt

deuten to point
er deutet

sich drehen to turn
er dreht sich (around)

drücken to press
er drückt

eilen to rush
er eilt

ein/frieren to freeze
er friert ein (food)

ein/laden to invite
ich lade ein
er lädt ein

ein/laufen to shrink
er läuft ein (clothes)
sie laufen ein

entdecken to spot
er entdeckt

entkommen to escape
er entkommt

sich erinnern an
— to remember
er erinnert
  sich an

erklären to explain
er erklärt

erzählen to tell
er erzählt (a story)

essen to eat
ich esse
er isst

* See *haben* for the other parts of this verb.   100

fahren ich fahre er fährt	to go (by car, boat, train), to drive
fallen ich falle er fällt	to fall
fallen lassen ich lasse fallen er lässt fallen	to drop
fangen ich fange er fängt	to catch
fegen er fegt	to sweep
fertig machen er macht fertig	to finish
fest/machen er macht fest	to fix (attach)
finden er findet	to find, to think (consider)
flicken er flickt	to mend, to repair
fliegen er fliegt	to fly
fragen er fragt	to ask
fressen ich fresse er frisst	to eat (of animals)
sich freuen er freut sich	to be glad
frieren er friert	to freeze
fühlen er fühlt	to feel (touch)
sich fühlen er fühlt sich	to feel (happy, sad)
führen er führt	to lead
füllen er füllt	to fill
funktionieren er funktioniert	to work (function)
füttern er füttert	to feed
gähnen er gähnt	to yawn
geben ich gebe er gibt	to give
gefrieren er gefriert	to freeze
gegenüber/stehen er steht gegenüber	to face
gehen er geht	to go (on foot)
gehören er gehört	to belong
gewinnen er gewinnt	to win
glauben er glaubt	to think
graben ich grabe er gräbt	to dig
haben ich habe du hast er, sie, es hat wir haben ihr habt sie haben Sie haben	to have
halten ich halte er hält	to hold
hängen er hängt	to hang
hassen er hasst	to hate
heizen er heizt	to heat (a room)
helfen ich helfe er hilft	to help
heran/reichen er reicht heran	to reach
hinauf/steigen er steigt hinauf	to climb
hin/fallen ich falle hin er fällt hin	to fall down
sich hin/knien er kniet sich hin	to kneel (down)
sich hin/legen er legt sich hin	to lie down
sich hin/setzen er setzt sich hin	to sit down
hinzu/fügen er fügt hinzu	to add (things)
hoch/heben er hebt hoch	to lift
hören er hört	to hear
hüpfen er hüpft	to hop
jagen er jagt	to chase, to hunt
jonglieren er jongliert	to juggle
jucken er juckt	to itch
kämpfen er kämpft	to fight
kaputt/machen er macht kaputt	to break (a machine)
kaufen er kauft	to buy
kehren er kehrt	to sweep
kennen er kennt	to know (people)
kicken er kickt	to kick
kleben er klebt	to stick
klingeln er klingelt	to ring
klopfen er klopft	to knock (on door)
knien er kniet	to kneel (be kneeling)
kochen er kocht	to cook
kommen er kommt	to come
können ich kann du kannst er, sie, es kann wir können ihr könnt sie können Sie können	to be able (I can, etc.)
krabbeln er krabbelt	to crawl (baby)
kriechen er kriecht	to crawl
küssen er küsst	to kiss
lächeln er lächelt	to smile
lachen er lacht	to laugh
lassen ich lasse er lässt	to let
laufen ich laufe er läuft	to walk, to run, to go on foot
läuten er läutet	to ring
leben er lebt	to live (be alive)
lecken er leckt	to lick
legen er legt	to put
lernen er lernt	to learn, to study
lesen ich lese er liest	to read

Verbs

lieben	to love	sich neigen	to lean	rufen	to call,	sehen	to see
er liebt		er neigt sich	(to one	er ruft	to shout	ich sehe	
			side)			er sieht	
liegen	to lie			rutschen	to slide		
er liegt	(be lying)	nennen	to call	er rutscht		sein	to be
		er nennt	(name)			ich bin	
liegen lassen	to leave			sagen	to say,	du bist	
ich lasse liegen	(some-	nicken	to nod	er sagt	to tell	er, sie, es ist	
er lässt liegen	thing)	er nickt				wir sind	
				schaukeln	to swing	ihr seid	
lügen	to lie	öffnen	to open	er schaukelt		sie sind	
er lügt	(tell a lie)	er öffnet				Sie sind	
				schenken	to give		
machen	to make,	parken	to park	er schenkt	(as a gift)	setzen	to put
er macht	to do	er parkt				er setzt	
				schicken	to send		
malen	to paint	passen	to fit	er schickt		singen	to sing
er malt	(a picture)	er passt				er singt	
				schieben	to push		
meinen	to think	passieren	to happen	er schiebt		sinken	to sink
er meint	(consider)	es passiert				er sinkt	
				schlafen	to sleep,		
messen	to measure	pflücken	to pick	ich schlafe	to be	sitzen	to sit
ich messe		er pflückt	(fruit or	er schläft	asleep	er sitzt	
er misst			flowers)				
				schlagen	to hit	sparen	to save
mischen	to mix	planen	to plan	ich schlage		er spart	(time, money)
er mischt		er plant		er schlägt			
						spielen	to play
mit/nehmen	to take	probieren	to try,	sich schlagen	to fight	er spielt	
ich nehme mit		er probiert	to taste	ich schlage mich			
er nimmt mit				er schlägt sich		sprechen	to speak,
		putzen	to clean			ich spreche	to talk
mögen	to like	er putzt		schleichen	to creep	er spricht	
ich mag				er schleicht			
du magst		quaken	to quack			springen	to jump,
er, sie, es mag		er quakt		schließen	to close,	er springt	to dive
wir mögen				er schließt	to shut		
ihr mögt		raten	to guess			spritzen	to splash
sie mögen		ich rate		schmecken	to taste	er spritzt	
Sie mögen		er rät		er schmeckt			
						stechen	to sting
müssen	to have to,	regnen	to rain	schneiden	to cut	ich steche	
ich muss	to need to	es regnet		er schneidet		er sticht	
du musst	(I must, etc.)						
er, sie, es muss		reichen	to pass	schneien	to snow	stecken	to put
wir müssen		er reicht	(give)	es schneit		er steckt	(inside)
ihr müsst							
sie müssen		reiten	to ride	schreiben	to write	stehen	to stand
Sie müssen		er reitet	(a horse)	er schreibt		er steht	
nach/ahmen	to copy	rennen	to run	schreien	to shout	stellen	to put
er ahmt nach	(actions)	er rennt		er schreit		er stellt	
nähen	to sew	reparieren	to fix,	schütteln	to shake	sterben	to die
er näht		er repariert	to mend	er schüttelt		ich sterbe	
						er stirbt	
		retten	to save,	schweben	to float		
nehmen	to take	er rettet	to rescue	er schwebt	(in air)	stoßen	to bump
ich nehme						ich stoße	
er nimmt		riechen	to smell	schwimmen	to swim,	er stößt	
		er riecht		er schwimmt	to float		

streichen — to paint (a room) er streicht	sich unterhalten — to talk ich unterhalte mich er unterhält sich	sich verstecken — to hide (yourself) er versteckt sich	wissen — to know (facts) ich weiß du weißt er, sie, es, weiß wir wissen ihr wisst sie wissen Sie wissen
sich stützen — to lean (on) er stützt sich	unterschreiben — to sign er unterschreibt	verstehen — to understand er versteht	
suchen — to search er sucht	sich verabschieden — to say goodbye er verabschiedet sich	versuchen — to try er versucht	wohnen — to live er wohnt
tanzen — to dance er tanzt	verbinden — to join (attach) er verbindet	voran/gehen — to lead (go ahead) er geht voran	wollen — to want ich will du willst er, sie, es will wir wollen ihr wollt sie wollen Sie wollen
tauchen — to dive er taucht	verbrennen — to burn er verbrennt	vorbei/gehen — to pass (go past) er geht vorbei	
teilen — to share er teilt	verbringen — to spend (time) er verbringt	wachsen — to grow (get bigger) ich wachse er wächst	
töten — to kill er tötet	vergessen — to forget ich vergesse er vergisst	wählen — to choose er wählt	zahlen — to pay er zahlt
tragen — to carry, to wear ich trage er trägt	verkaufen — to sell er verkauft	warten — to wait er wartet	zeichnen — to draw er zeichnet
träumen — to dream er träumt	verlassen — to leave (a place, a person) ich verlasse er verlässt	waschen — to wash ich wasche er wäscht	zeigen — to show, to point er zeigt
sich treffen — to meet ich treffe mich er trifft sich	verlieren — to lose er verliert	sich waschen — to wash (yourself) ich wasche mich er wäscht sich	zelten — to camp er zeltet
trinken — to drink er trinkt	vermissen — to miss (someone) er vermisst	wecken — to wake (someone) er weckt	zerbrechen — to break ich zerbreche er zerbricht
trocknen — to dry er trocknet	verpassen — to miss (train, bus) er verpasst	weg/nehmen — to take (away) ich nehme weg er nimmt weg	ziehen — to pull, to grow (cultivate) er zieht
tun — to do ich tue du tust er, sie, es tut wir tun ihr tut sie tun Sie tun	verrühren — to stir, to mix er verrührt	weh/tun* — to hurt er tut weh	zu/machen — to close, to shut er macht zu
	verschütten — to spill er verschüttet	weinen — to cry er weint	zusammen/falten — to fold er faltet zusammen
überqueren — to cross er überquert	verschwinden — to disappear er verschwindet	werden — to become ich werde du wirst er, sie, es wird wir werden ihr werdet sie werden Sie werden	zusammen/passen — to match es passt zusammen
umarmen — to hug er umarmt	versprechen — to promise ich verspreche er verspricht		zusammen/zählen — to add (numbers) er zählt zusammen
um/stellen — to move (an object) er stellt um			
um/stoßen — to knock (over) ich stoße um er stößt um	versprintzen — to splash er verspritzt	werfen — to throw ich werfe er wirft	zu/werfen — to throw (to someone) ich werfe zu er wirft zu
unter/gehen — to sink er geht unter	verstecken — to hide (things) er versteckt	winken — to wave er winkt	zu/winken — to wave (to someone) er winkt zu

* See *tun* for the other parts of this verb.   103

Complete German word list

Plurals of nouns are shown in parentheses. Nouns that don't change their spelling in the plural are shown like this: der Eimer (-)

ab/biegen	to turn (left or right)
der Abend (-e)	evening
das Abendessen (-)	dinner
abends	in the evening
aber	but
ab/lecken	to lick (of animals)
ab/schreiben	to copy (writing)
sich ab/trocknen	to dry yourself
acht	eight
acht-	eighth
achtzehn	eighteen
achtzig	eighty
der Adler (-)	eagle
die Adresse (-n)	address
der Affe (-n)	ape, monkey
alle	all, everybody, everyone
allein	alone
alles	everything
das Alphabet (-e)	alphabet
als	than, when (in past)
also	so (because of this)
alt	old
die Ameise (-n)	ant
sich amüsieren	to enjoy yourself
an	at (a place), on (something vertical)
die Ananas (-se)	pineapple
anbrennen lassen	to burn (food)
ander-	other
an/fangen	to start
angeln	to fish
Angst haben	to be afraid
an/haben	to wear
an/halten	to stop
an/kommen	to arrive, to reach
an/schauen	to look (at), to watch
an/sehen	to look (at), to watch
an sich drücken	to hug (toy, animal)
die Antwort (-en)	answer
antworten	to answer, to reply
an . . . vorbei	past
die Anzahl	number (amount)
an/ziehen	to dress (someone)
sich an/ziehen	to dress (yourself)
der Apfel (Äpfel)	apple
April	April
arbeiten	to work
das Arbeitszimmer (-)	study
arm	poor
der Arm (-e)	arm
die Armbanduhr (-en)	watch
der Ärmel (-)	sleeve
die Art (-en)	kind, sort, way (method)
artig	good (well-behaved)
der Arzt (Ärzte)	doctor (man)
die Ärztin (-nen)	doctor (woman)
der Astronaut (-en)	astronaut (man)
die Astronautin (-nen)	astronaut (woman)
atmen	to breathe
auch	also, too
auf	on (something flat)
auf/bewahren	to keep (store)
auf einmal	suddenly
aufgeregt	upset (worried)
auf/hören	to stop (doing something)
auf/machen	to open
auf/stehen	to stand up
auf/wachen	to wake up
auf/wärmen	to heat (food)
auf Wiedersehen	goodbye
das Auge (-n)	eye
August	August
aus/geben	to spend (money)
aus/machen	to matter, to turn off
aus/rutschen	to slip
aus/schneiden	to cut out
aus/schütten	to spill
außen	outside (outdoors)
außerhalb	outside (something)
die Aussicht (-en)	view
aus/suchen	to choose, to pick
aus/ziehen	to undress (someone)
sich aus/ziehen	to undress (yourself)
das Auto (-s)	car
das Baby (-s)	baby
backen	to bake
der Bäcker (-)	baker (man)
die Bäckerin (-nen)	baker (woman)
der Badeanzug (Badeanzüge)	swimsuit
das Badetuch (Badetücher)	towel (bath, beach)
die Badewanne (-n)	bathtub
der Bagger (-)	digger
der Bahnhof (Bahnhöfe)	station
balancieren	to balance
bald	soon
der Ball (Bälle)	ball
die Balletttänzerin (-nen)	ballerina
der Ballon (-s)	(hot-air) balloon
die Banane (-n)	banana
das Band (Bänder)	ribbon
die Band (-s)	band (music)
die Bank (-en)	bank
der Bär (-en)	bear
der Bart (Bärte)	beard
bauen	to build
der Bauer (-n)	farmer
der Bauernhof (Bauernhöfe)	farm
der Baum (Bäume)	tree
der Baumstamm (Baumstämme)	log
sich bedanken	to thank
bedeuten	to mean
sich beeilen	to hurry, to rush
sich befassen mit	to study (a topic)
befühlen	to feel (touch)
begegnen	to meet (by chance)
beginnen	to begin
behalten	to keep
bei	at (a place)
das Bein (-e)	leg
beißen	to bite
das belegte Brot	sandwich
bellen	to bark
bemerken	to notice
benutzen	to use
bereit	ready
der Berg (-e)	mountain
berühren	to touch
beschäftigt	busy
besichtigen	to visit (a place)
besonder-	special
bestimmt	special, certain
bestürzt	upset (sad)
besuchen	to visit, to see (visit)
betrübt	upset (sad)
das Bett (-en)	bed
das Bettlaken (-)	sheet (on bed)
sich bewegen	to move (yourself)
bezahlen	to pay for
die Biene (-n)	bee
das Bild (-er)	picture
billig	cheap
binden	to tie
der Bindfaden	string
die Birne (-n)	pear
bis	until
bitte	please
blasen	to blow
blass	pale
das Blatt (Blätter)	leaf, sheet (of paper)
blau	blue
bleiben	to stay (remain)
der Bleistift (-e)	pencil
der Blick (-e)	view
die Blockflöte (-n)	recorder
bloß	only
die Blume (-n)	flower
der Blumenkohl (-e)	cauliflower
der Boden (Böden)	floor, ground
die Bohne (-n)	bean
das Boot (-e)	boat
böse	angry
braten	to fry
brauchen	to need
braun	brown
brav	good (well-behaved)
brechen	to break
breit	wide
brennen	to burn
der Brief (-e)	letter
die Briefmarke (-n)	stamp
die Brille (-n)	glasses
bringen	to bring
das Brot (-e)	bread
die Brücke (-n)	bridge

der Bruder (Brüder)	brother
das Buch (Bücher)	book
buchstabieren	to spell
das Bügeleisen (-)	iron
bügeln	to iron
die Burg (-en)	castle
die Bürste (-n)	brush
der Bus (-se)	bus
der Busch (Büsche)	bush
die Butter	butter
das Café (-s)	café
die CD (-s)	CD
der Clown (-s)	clown
der Computer (-)	computer
der Cousin (-s)	cousin (boy)
die Cousine (-n)	cousin (girl)
da	there, since (because)
das Dach (Dächer)	roof
dahin	(to) there
damals	then (at that time)
die Dame (-n)	lady
danach	next (after that)
danken	to thank
dann	then, next
das Datum (Daten)	date
der Daumen (-)	thumb
die Decke (-n)	blanket
der Deckel (-)	lid
der Delphin (-e)	dolphin
denken	to think
der-, die-, dasselbe	the same
deuten	to point
Dezember	December
dick	fat
Dienstag	Tuesday
das Ding (-e)	thing
der Dinosaurier (-)	dinosaur
Donnerstag	Thursday
dort	there
dorthin	(to) there
der Drache (-n)	dragon
der Drachen (-)	kite
draußen	outside
der Dreck	mess, dirt
sich drehen	to turn (around)
drei	three
das Dreieck (-e)	triangle
dreißig	thirty
dreizehn	thirteen
dritt-	third
drücken	to press
der Dschungel (-)	jungle
dunkel	dark
dünn	thin
durch	through
das Durcheinander	mess (untidy)
Durst haben	to be thirsty
die Dusche (-n)	shower (for washing)

echt	real (not artificial)
das Ei (-er)	egg
das Eichhörnchen (-)	squirrel
eigen	own
eilen	to rush (move quickly)
der Eimer (-)	bucket
ein/frieren	to freeze (food)
einige	some
ein/laden	to invite
die Einladung (-en)	invitation
ein/laufen	to shrink (clothes)
einmal	once
eins	one
das Eis	ice, ice cream
der Elefant (-en)	elephant
elf	eleven
der Ellbogen (-)	elbow
die Eltern	parents
die E-Mail	email
das Ende (-n)	end, tip (of tail)
eng	narrow
der Engel (-)	angel
das Enkelkind (-er)	grandchild
entdecken	to spot
die Ente (-n)	duck
das Entenküken (-)	duckling
entkommen	to escape
die Erbse (-n)	pea
die Erdbeere (-n)	strawberry
die Erde	earth, soil
die Erdnuss (Erdnüsse)	peanut
sich erinnern an	to remember
die Erkältung (-en)	cold
erklären	to explain
erst-	first
der Erwachsene	adult, grown-up
erzählen	to tell (a story)
der Esel (-)	donkey
essen	to eat
das Essen (-)	food, meal
etwas	something, some, anything
etwas gegen . . . haben	to mind
die Eule (-n)	owl
die Fahne (-n)	flag
fahren	to go, to drive, to ride (a bicycle)
die Fahrkarte (-n)	ticket (train, bus)
das Fahrrad (Fahrräder)	bicycle
die Fahrt (-en)	journey
fallen	to fall
fallen lassen	to drop
der Fallschirm (-e)	parachute
falsch	wrong (incorrect)
die Familie (-n)	family
fangen	to catch
die Farbe (-n)	color, paint
fast	almost

faul	lazy, bad (fruit, vegetables)
Februar	February
die Fee (-n)	fairy
fegen	to sweep
der Fehler (-)	mistake
die Feier (-n)	party
das Feld (-er)	field (for crops)
das Fell (-e)	fur
der Fels (-en)	rock (stone)
das Fenster (-)	window
das Fernsehen	television, TV
der Fernseher (-)	television (set), TV (set)
fertig	ready
fertig machen	to finish
fertig sein	to have finished
fest/machen	to fix (attach)
fett	fat
das Feuer (-)	fire
das Feuerwehrauto (-s)	fire engine
die Feuerwehrfrau (-en)	firefighter (woman)
der Feuerwehrmann (Feuerwehrmänner)	firefighter (man)
finden	to find, to think (consider)
der Finger (-)	finger
der Fisch (-e)	fish
fit	fit (healthy)
flach	flat
die Flasche (-n)	bottle
der Fleck (-e or -en)	spot
die Fledermaus (Fledermäuse)	bat (animal)
das Fleisch	meat
flicken	to mend, to repair
die Fliege (-n)	fly (insect)
fliegen	to fly
das Flugzeug (-e)	plane
der Fluss (Flüsse)	river
das Fohlen (-)	foal
die Form (-en)	shape
das Foto (-s)	photo
das Fotoalbum (Fotoalben)	photo album
der Fotoapparat (-e)	camera
die Frage (-n)	question
fragen	to ask
die Frau (-en)	woman
frech	naughty, bad
frei	free (not restricted)
Freitag	Friday
fressen	to eat (of animals)
sich freuen	to be glad
der Freund (-e)	friend (boy)
die Freundin (-nen)	friend (girl)
freundlich	friendly
frieren	to freeze
frisch	fresh
der Frosch (Frösche)	frog

German word list

früh	early	der Gipfel (-)	peak (mountain)	helfen	to help
der Frühling	spring	die Giraffe (-n)	giraffe	hell	bright (light), light (color)
das Frühstück (-e)	breakfast	die Gitarre (-n)	guitar		
der Fuchs (Füchse)	fox	das Glas (Gläser)	glass, jar	der Helm (-e)	helmet
fühlen	to feel (touch)	glatt	smooth, straight (hair)	das Hemd (-en)	shirt
sich fühlen	to feel (happy, sad)	eine Glatze haben	to be bald	die Henne (-n)	hen
führen	to lead	glauben	to think	heran/reichen	to reach
füllen	to fill	gleich	equal, same	der Herbst	fall (season)
der Füller (-)	pen (ink)	glücklich	happy	herein	inside, in
fünf	five	das Gold	gold	herunter	down
fünft-	fifth	golden	gold (golden)	das Herz (-en)	heart
fünfzehn	fifteen	graben	to dig	heute	today
fünfzig	fifty	die Grapefruit (-s)	grapefruit	heute Abend	this evening, tonight
funktionieren	to work (function)	das Gras	grass	heute Nacht	tonight (in the night)
für	for	gratis	free (no cost)	die Hexe (-n)	witch
der Fuß (Füße)	foot, base	grau	gray	hier	here
der Fußball	soccer	der Griff (-e)	handle	hierher	(to) here
füttern	to feed	groß	big, large, tall (person), great	die Himbeere (-n)	raspberry
				der Himmel	sky
die Gabel (-n)	fork	die Größe (-n)	height, size	hinauf/steigen	to climb
gähnen	to yawn	die Großeltern	grandparents	hinein	inside, in
die Gans (Gänse)	goose	die Großmutter		hin/fallen	to fall over
ganz	quite (completely)	(Großmütter)	grandmother	sich hin/knien	to kneel (down)
der Garten (Gärten)	garden	die Großstadt (Großstädte)	city	sich hin/legen	to lie (down)
das Gas (-e)	gas	der Großvater		sich hin/setzen	to sit (down)
der Gast (Gäste)	guest, visitor	(Großväter)	grandfather	hinten	at the back
das Gebäude (-)	building	grün	green	hinter	behind, at the back of
geben	to give	die Gruppe (-n)	group	hinunter	down
der Geburtstag (-e)	birthday	die Gurke (-n)	cucumber	hinzu/fügen	to add (things)
das Gedicht (-e)	poem	der Gürtel (-)	belt	der Hirsch (-e)	deer
gefährlich	dangerous	gut	good, well	hoch	high, tall (building)
gefrieren	to freeze			hoch/heben	to lift
der Gefrierschrank (Gefrierschränke)	freezer	die Haarbürste (-n)	hairbrush	der Hochstuhl (Hochstühle)	highchair
gegen . . . fahren	to crash into	die Haare	hair	der Hocker (-)	stool
der Gegensatz (Gegensätze)	opposite	haben	to have	hoh-	high, tall (building)
gegenüber	opposite (facing)	das Hähnchen (-)	chicken (cooked)	die Höhe (-n)	height (house, mountain)
gegenüber/stehen	to face	der Hai (-e)	shark	die Höhle (-n)	cave
das Geheimnis (-se)	secret	halb	half	das Holz	wood
gehen	to go (on foot)	der Halbmond (-e)	crescent	das Holzscheit (-e)	log (for fire)
gehören	to belong	die Hälfte (-n)	half (portion)	der Honig	honey
gelb	yellow	hallo	hello	hören	to hear
das Geld	money	der Hals (Hälse)	neck	der Hotdog (-s)	hotdog
das Gemüse	vegetables	die Halskette (-n)	necklace	das Hotel (-s)	hotel
geöffnet	open	halten	to hold	hübsch	pretty
gerade	straight (line), even (number), upright (person)	der Hamburger (-)	burger, hamburger	der Hubschrauber (-)	helicopter
		der Hammer (Hämmer)	hammer	der Hügel (-)	hill
das Geräusch (-e)	noise, sound	der Hamster (-)	hamster	das Huhn (Hühner)	hen
gern	with pleasure, gladly	die Hand (Hände)	hand	der Hund (-e)	dog
geröntgt werden	to have an x-ray	der Handschuh (-e)	glove	das Hündchen (-)	puppy
das Geschenk (-e)	present, gift	das Handtuch (Handtücher)	towel	hundert	hundred
die Geschichte (-n)	story	hängen	to hang	Hunger haben	to be hungry
das Gesicht (-er)	face	hart	hard (surface)	hüpfen	to hop
das Gespenst (-er)	ghost	hassen	to hate	der Hut (Hüte)	hat
gestern	yesterday	hässlich	ugly		
das Getränk (-e)	drink	der, die, das Haupt-	main	die Idee (-n)	idea
die Getreideflocken	cereal	das Haus (Häuser)	house	immer	always
gewinnen	to win	der Hausschuh (-e)	slipper	in	inside, in, into
gewöhnlich	usually, usual	das Haustier (-e)	pet	das Insekt (-en)	insect
		die Haut	skin	die Insel (-n)	island
		heiß	hot	das Internet	Internet, Net, World Wide Web
		heizen	to heat (a room)		

irgendwo	somewhere, anywhere	kleiner werden	to shrink	das Lamm	
		das Kleinkind (-er)	toddler	(Lämmer)	lamb
ja	yes	klingeln	to ring	die Lampe (-n)	lamp
die Jacke (-n)	jacket	die Klinke (-n)	handle (door)	das Land (Länder)	country, land
jagen	to chase, to hunt	klopfen	to knock (on a	die Landkarte (-n)	map
das Jahr (-e)	year		door)	lang	long
die Jahreszeit (-en)	season	knall-	bright (color)	die Länge (-n)	length
Januar	January	das Knie (-)	knee	langsam	slow, slowly
die Jeans	jeans	knien	to kneel (be	langweilig	dull (boring)
jeder, jede, jedes	each, every		kneeling)	der Lärm	noise (loud)
jemand	somebody, someone,	der Knöchel (-)	ankle	lassen	to let
	anybody, anyone	der Knochen (-)	bone	der Lastwagen (-)	truck
jetzt	now	der Knopf		das Lätzchen (-)	bib
der Job (-s)	job	(Knöpfe)	button	laufen	to walk, to run, to
jonglieren	to juggle	der Knoten (-)	knot		rush (move quickly)
jucken	to itch	der Koch (Köche)	chef (man)	laut	loud, noisy
Juli	July	kochen	to cook	läuten	to ring
jung	young	die Köchin (-nen)	chef (woman)	leben	to live (be alive)
der Junge (-n)	boy	der Koffer (-)	suitcase	das Leben (-)	life
Juni	June	komisch	funny (strange)	die Lebensmittel	food (groceries)
		kommen	to come	lecken	to lick
der Käfer (-)	beetle, bug	der König (-e)	king	lecker	delicious
der Kaffee	coffee	die Königin (-nen)	queen	leer	empty
der Käfig (-e)	cage	der Kopf (Köpfe)	head	legen	to put
das Kalb (Kälber)	calf	das Kopfkissen (-)	pillow	der Lehrer (-)	teacher (man)
kalt	cold	der Kopfsalat (-e)	lettuce	die Lehrerin (-nen)	teacher (woman)
das Kamel (-e)	camel	der Korb (Körbe)	basket	leicht	easy, light (not
der Kamm		der Körper (-)	body		heavy)
(Kämme)	comb	kostenlos	free (no cost)	leise	quiet
kämpfen	to fight	krabbeln	to crawl (baby)	die Leiter (-n)	ladder
das Känguru (-s)	kangaroo	kräftig	strong	lernen	to learn, to study
das Kaninchen (-)	rabbit	das Krankenhaus		lesen	to read
die Kante (-n)	edge	(Krankenhäuser)	hospital	letzt-	last
kaputt/machen	to break (machine)	die Kranken-		die Leute	people
die Karotte (-n)	carrot	schwester (-n)	nurse	das Licht (-er)	light
die Karte (-n)	card, map, ticket	der Kranken-		lieb (lieber, liebe)	dear, kind, friendly
die Kartoffel (-n)	potato	wagen (-)	ambulance	lieben	to love
der Karton (-s)	box (cardboard)	die Kreide	chalk	das Lied (-er)	song
der Käse	cheese	der Kreis (-e)	circle	liegen	to lie (be lying
das Kätzchen (-)	kitten	das Kreuz (-e)	cross, x		down)
die Katze (-n)	cat	kriechen	to crawl	liegen lassen	to leave (something)
kaufen	to buy	das Krokodil (-e)	crocodile	das Lineal (-e)	ruler
kehren	to sweep	die Krone (-n)	crown	die Linie (-n)	line (on paper)
kein, keine, kein,		die Küche (-n)	kitchen	link-	left (not right)
keine	no (not any)	der Kuchen (-)	cake	links	left (not right)
der Kellner (-)	waiter	der Kugelschreiber		die Lippe (-n)	lip
die Kellnerin (-nen)	waitress	(-)	pen (ballpoint)	die Liste (-n)	list
kennen	to know (people)	die Kuh (Kühe)	cow	das Loch	
die Kerze (-n)	candle	der Kühlschrank		(Löcher)	hole
kicken	to kick	(Kühlschränke)	refrigerator	der Löffel (-)	spoon
der Kieselstein (-e)	pebble	das Küken (-)	chick	los sein	to happen
das Kind (-er)	child	der Kuli (-s)	pen (ballpoint)	der Löwe (-n)	lion
das Kinn (-e)	chin	die Kunst	art	die Luft	air
die Kirsche (-n)	cherry	der Künstler (-)	artist (man)	der Luftballon (-s)	balloon
die Kiste (-n)	box (big)	die Künstlerin		lügen	to lie (tell a lie)
die Klasse (-n)	class	(-nen)	artist (woman)	lustig	funny (amusing)
das Klassenzimmer		der Kürbis (-se)	pumpkin		
(-)	classroom	kurz	short	machen	to do, to make
das Klavier (-e)	piano	die kurze Hose	shorts	das Mädchen (-)	girl
kleben	to stick	der Kuss (Küsse)	kiss	die Mahlzeit (-en)	meal
der Klebstoff (-e)	glue	küssen	to kiss	Mai	May
das Kleid (-er)	dress			malen	to paint (a picture)
die Kleider	clothes	lächeln	to smile	manchmal	sometimes
klein	small, young	lachen	to laugh	der Mann	
	(children)	der Lack	paint (on metal)	(Männer)	man

German word list

die Mannschaft (-en)	team
der Mantel (Mäntel)	coat
der Marienkäfer (-)	ladybug
die Marionette (-n)	puppet (on strings)
der Markt (Märkte)	market
März	March
die Maschine (-n)	machine
das Match (-e)	match (game)
der Matrose (-n)	sailor (man)
die Matrosin (-nen)	sailor (woman)
matt	dull (color)
die Mauer (-n)	wall (outside)
die Maus (Mäuse)	mouse
das Medikament (-e)	medicine
das Meer (-e)	sea
das Meer- schweinchen (-)	guinea pig
das Mehl	flour
mehr	more
meinen	to think
meist-	most
die Menge (-n)	amount
der Mensch (-en)	person
messen	to measure
das Messer (-)	knife
das Metall (-e)	metal
der Metzger (-)	butcher
die Mikrowelle (-n)	microwave
die Milch	milk
die Minute (-n)	minute
mischen	to mix
mit	with, by (car, bus)
Mitglied werden	to join (a club)
mit/nehmen	to take
das Mittagessen (-)	lunch
die Mitte	middle
das Mittel (-)	medicine
mitten	in the middle, in the center
Mittwoch	Wednesday
das Modell (-e)	model
mögen	to like
der Monat (-e)	month
der Mond (-e)	moon
Montag	Monday
morgen	tomorrow
der Morgen (-)	morning
das Motorrad (Motorräder)	motorcycle
der Motorroller (-)	scooter (with motor)
der Mund (Münder)	mouth
die Münze (-n)	coin
die Muschel (-n)	shell (sea)
die Musik	music
müssen	to need to, to have to
die Mutter (Mütter)	mother
Mutti	Mom
die Mütze (-n)	cap

nach	after, to (a town or country)
nach/ahmen	to copy (actions)
der Nachbar (-n)	neighbor (man)
die Nachbarin (-nen)	neighbor (woman)
der Nachmittag (-e)	afternoon
nachmittags	in the afternoon
die Nachricht (-en)	news, message
nächst-	next
die Nacht (Nächte)	night
der Nachtfalter (-)	moth
nackt	bare
die Nacktschnecke (-n)	slug
die Nadel (-n)	needle
der Nagel (Nägel)	nail
nahe	close
in der Nähe (von)	close (to)
nähen	to sew
der Name (-n)	name
die Nase (-n)	nose
das Nashorn (Nashörner)	rhinoceros, rhino
nass	wet
die Natur	nature
neben	beside, next to, by
nehmen	to take
sich neigen	to lean (to one side)
nein	no
nennen	to call (name)
das Nest (-er)	nest
nett	nice, kind, friendly
das Netz (-e)	net, web (spider's)
neu	new
das Neueste	news
neun	nine
neunt-	ninth
neunzehn	nineteen
neunzig	ninety
nicht	not
nicht leiden können	to hate
nichts	nothing
nicht tief	shallow, not deep
nicken	to nod
nie	never
niedlich	cute, sweet
niedrig	low
niemand	no one
das Nilpferd (-e)	hippopotamus, hippo
nirgends	nowhere
noch	still, yet
noch ein, eine, ein	another
noch einmal	again, once more
normalerweise	usually
die Note (-n)	note (music)
die Notiz (-en)	note (message)
das Notizbuch (Notizbücher)	notebook
November	November
null	zero
die Nummer (-n)	number (street, phone)
nur	only

die Nuss (Nüsse)	nut
nützlich	useful
oben	on top
das Obst	fruit
oder	or
offen	open
öffnen	to open
oft	often
ohne	without
das Ohr (-en)	ear
Oktober	October
das Öl	oil
Oma	Granny
der Onkel (-)	uncle
Opa	Grandpa
die Orange (-n)	orange (fruit)
orangefarben	orange (color)
der Ort (-e)	place
das Oval (-e)	oval
der Ozean (-e)	ocean
das Paar (-e)	pair
ein paar	some
der Palast (Paläste)	palace
der Papagei (-en)	parrot
das Papier (-e)	paper
die Paprikaschote (-n)	pepper (vegetable)
der Park (-s or -e)	park
parken	to park
die Party (-s)	party
passen	to fit
passieren	to happen
der Pelz (-e)	fur
die Person (-en)	person
der Pfad (-e)	path
der Pfeffer	pepper (spice)
das Pferd (-e)	horse
der Pfirsich (-e)	peach
die Pflanze (-n)	plant
die Pflaume (-n)	plum
pflücken	to pick (flowers, fruit)
die Pfote (-n)	paw
die Pfütze (-n)	puddle
das Picknick (-e or -s)	picnic
der Pilot (-en)	pilot (man)
die Pilotin (-nen)	pilot (woman)
der Pilz (-e)	mushroom
der Pinguin (-e)	penguin
die Pizza (Pizzas or Pizzen)	pizza
der Plan (Pläne)	plan
planen	to plan
der Planet (-en)	planet
der Platz (Plätze)	place, space, room, seat
plötzlich	suddenly
der Po (-s)	bottom
die Polizei	police
das Polizeiauto (-s)	police car
das Pony (-s)	pony
der Preis (-e)	price, prize
der Prinz (-en)	prince

die Prinzessin (-nen)	princess
probieren	to try, to taste (take a little)
der Punkt (-e)	point (score), spot
die Puppe (-n)	doll, puppet
putzen	to clean
das Puzzle (-s)	jigsaw puzzle
das Quadrat (-e)	square
quaken	to quack
das Quiz (-)	quiz
das Rad (Räder)	wheel, bicycle
mit dem Rad fahren	to cycle, to ride a bike
das Radio (-s)	radio
die Rakete (-n)	rocket
der Rand (Ränder)	edge
raten	to guess
das Rätsel (-)	puzzle (wordgame)
die Ratte (-n)	rat
das Raumfahrzeug (-e)	spacecraft
die Raupe (-n)	caterpillar
die Rechen- aufgabe (-n)	sum (math), math problem
recht-	right (not left)
das Rechteck (-e)	rectangle
rechts	right (not left)
das Regal (-e)	shelf
der Regen	rain
der Regenbogen (-)	rainbow
der Regenschirm (-e)	umbrella
regnen	to rain
reich	rich
reichen	to pass (give)
reif	ripe
die Reihe (-n)	line (of people)
der Reis	rice
die Reise (-n)	journey
der Reißverschluss (Reißverschlüsse)	zipper
reiten	to ride (a horse)
rennen	to run
reparieren	to fix, to mend, to repair
retten	to save (from danger), to rescue
richtig	right, true
richtig schreiben können	to spell
riechen	to smell
der Riese (-n)	giant
riesig	enormous
die Rinde (-n)	bark (of tree)
der Ring (-e)	ring
der Ritter (-)	knight
der Roboter (-)	robot
der Rock (Röcke)	skirt
die Rockmusik	rock (music)

der Roller (-)	scooter
Rollschuh laufen	to skate (on rollerskates)
das Röntgenbild (-er)	x-ray
rosa	pink
die Rose (-n)	rose
die Rosine (-n)	raisin
rot	red
die Rote Bete	beetroot
der Rücken (-)	back
rufen	to call, to shout
ruhig	quiet, calm
rund	round
die Rutschbahn (-en)	slide
rutschen	to slide
die Sache (-n)	thing
der Saft (Säfte)	juice
die Säge (-n)	saw
sagen	to say, to tell
die Salami	salami
der Salat (-e)	salad
das Salz	salt
Samstag	Saturday
der Sand	sand
die Sandale (-n)	sandal
sanft	gentle
satt	full (after eating)
der Sattel (Sättel)	saddle
der Satz (Sätze)	sentence
sauber	clean
die Schachtel (-n)	box (small)
das Schaf (-e)	sheep
der Schal (-s or -e)	scarf
die Schale (-n)	skin (fruit, vegetable), shell (eggs, nuts)
scharf	sharp (edge)
der Schatten (-)	shadow
der Schauer (-)	shower (of rain)
die Schaukel (-n)	swing
schaukeln	to swing
der Schauspieler (-)	actor
die Schauspielerin (-nen)	actress
die Scheibe (-n)	slice
schenken	to give (as a gift)
die Schere (-n)	scissors
die Scheune (-n)	barn
schicken	to send
schieben	to push
das Schiff (-e)	ship
das Schild (-er)	sign (on road)
der Schild (-e)	peak (on cap)
der Schirm (-e)	peak (on cap)
schlafen	to sleep, to be asleep
das Schlafzimmer (-)	bedroom
schlagen	to hit
sich schlagen mit	to fight
der Schläger (-)	bat (for sports)
der Schlamm	mud
die Schlange (-n)	snake
schlecht	bad

schleichen	to creep
schließen	to close, to shut
Schlittschuh laufen	to skate (on ice)
das Schloss (Schlösser)	castle, palace, lock
der Schlüssel (-)	key
schmecken	to taste
der Schmetterling (-e)	butterfly
schmutzig	dirty
der Schnabel (Schnäbel)	beak
die Schnecke (-n)	snail
der Schnee	snow
schneiden	to cut
schneien	to snow
schnell	quick, fast
der Schnupfen (-)	cold
die Schokolade	chocolate
schön	beautiful, nice
schreiben	to write
der Schreibtisch (-e)	desk
schreien	to shout (very loudly)
der Schuh (-e)	shoe
die Schule (-n)	school
der Schüler (-)	pupil (boy)
die Schülerin (-nen)	pupil (girl)
der Schulhof (Schulhöfe)	playground (school)
die Schulter (-n)	shoulder
die Schüssel (-n)	bowl
schütteln	to shake
der Schwamm (Schwämme)	sponge
der Schwan (Schwäne)	swan
der Schwanz (Schwänze)	tail
schwarz	black
schweben	to float (in air)
schwer	heavy, difficult, hard
die Schwester (-n)	sister
schwierig	difficult, hard
das Schwimmbad (Schwimmbäder)	(swimming) pool
das Schwimm- becken (-)	(swimming) pool
schwimmen	to swim, to float
sechs	six
sechst-	sixth
sechzehn	sixteen
sechzig	sixty
der See (-n)	lake
die See	sea
der Seehund (-e)	seal
sehen	to see
sehr	very
sehr gern mögen	to love
seicht	shallow
die Seife	soap
das Seil (-e)	rope
seit	since (time)
die Seite (-n)	side, page
seltsam	odd (strange)

German word list

senkrecht	upright (wall, pillar)
September	September
setzen	to put
das Shampoo	shampoo
die Shorts	shorts
sicher	safe, sure
sieben	seven
siebt-	seventh
siebzehn	seventeen
siebzig	seventy
singen	to sing
sinken	to sink
der Sitz (-e)	seat (chair)
sitzen	to sit (be sitting)
Ski fahren	to ski
so	so (so big)
die Socke (-n)	sock
das Sofa (-s)	sofa
der Sohn (Söhne)	son
der Soldat (-en)	soldier
der Sommer	summer
die Sonne	sun
die Sonnenblume (-n)	sunflower
die Sonnenbrille (-n)	sunglasses
Sonntag	Sunday
die Sorte (-n)	kind, sort
sparen	to save (time, money)
der Spaß	fun
spät	late
der Spiegel (-)	mirror
ein Spiegelei machen	to fry an egg
das Spiel (-e)	game, match
spielen	to play
der Spielplatz (Spielplätze)	playground (in park)
die Spielsachen	toys
das Spielzeug (-e)	toy
der Spinat	spinach
die Spinne (-n)	spider
spitz	sharp (point)
die Spitze (-n)	tip, point
der Sport (-e)	sport
die Sprache (-n)	language
sprechen	to speak, to talk
springen	to jump, to dive
spritzen	to splash
das Spülbecken (-)	sink (kitchen)
stabil	strong (solid)
die Stadt (Städte)	town, city
die Stange (-n)	bar
der Star (-s)	star (person)
stark	strong
statt	instead of
der Staubsauger (-)	vacuum cleaner
stechen	to sting
stecken	to put (inside)
stehen	to stand
steil	steep
der Stein (-e)	stone, rock
die Stelle (-n)	place, job
stellen	to put
sterben	to die
der Stern (-e)	star (in sky)
der Stiefel (-)	boot
der Stiel (-e)	handle (of pan)
still	quiet, still
die Stimme (-n)	voice
der Stock (Stöcke)	stick
stoßen	to bump
der Strand (Strände)	beach
die Straße (-n)	street, road
streichen	to paint (a room)
das Streichholz (Streichhölzer)	match (for fire)
der Strom	electricity
das Stück (-e)	piece, slice (of cake)
der Stuhl (Stühle)	chair
die Stunde (-n)	hour, lesson
der Sturm (Stürme)	storm
sich stützen	to lean (on)
suchen	to search
die Summe (-n)	sum, math problem
der Supermarkt (Supermärkte)	supermarket
die Suppe (-n)	soup
süß	sweet
der Tag (-e)	day
die Tante (-n)	aunt
tanzen	to dance
tapfer	brave
die Tasche (-n)	bag, pocket
die Tasse (-n)	cup
die Tatsache (-n)	fact
tauchen	to dive (underwater)
der Taucher (-)	diver
tausend	thousand
das Taxi (-s)	taxi
der Teddy (-s)	teddy bear
der Tee	tea
der Teich (-e)	pond
das Teil (-e)	part, piece
teilen	to share
das Telefon (-e)	telephone, phone
der Teller (-)	plate
der Teppich (-e)	carpet, rug (big)
der Teppichboden (Teppichböden)	carpet
teuer	expensive
tief	deep
die Tiefkühltruhe (-n)	freezer
das Tier (-e)	animal
der Tiergarten (Tiergärten)	zoo
der Tiger (-)	tiger
der Tintenfisch (-e)	octopus
der Tisch (-e)	table
der Toast	toast
die Tochter (Töchter)	daughter
die Toilette (-n)	toilet
toll	great (fantastic)
die Tomate (-n)	tomato
der Ton (Töne)	sound
das Tor (-e)	gate, goal
töten	to kill
tragen	to carry, to wear
der Traktor (-en)	tractor
die Traube (-n)	grape
der Traum (Träume)	dream
träumen	to dream
traurig	sad
sich treffen	to meet (by arrangement)
die Treppe	stairs
trinken	to drink
trocken	dry
trocknen	to dry
die Trommel (-n)	drum
der Tropfen (-)	drop (of liquid)
der Truthahn (Truthähne)	turkey
das T-Shirt (-s)	T-shirt
tun	to do
tun als ob	to pretend
die Tür (-en)	door
die Tüte (-n)	bag (plastic, paper)
über	over, across, about (story)
überall	everywhere
überqueren	to cross
die Überraschung (-en)	surprise
die Überschwemmung (-en)	flood
Uhr	o'clock, time (what time is it?)
die Uhr (-en)	clock, watch
um	around, at (a time)
umarmen	to hug
der Umschlag (Umschläge)	envelope
umsonst	free (no cost)
um/stellen	to move (an object)
um/stoßen	to knock (over)
um . . . zu	to (in order to)
unartig	naughty
und	and
einen Unfall haben	to crash, to have an accident
ungefähr	about (roughly)
ungerade	uneven (number)
unglücklich	unhappy
unrecht	wrong (bad)
unten	at the bottom
unter	under, below
unter/gehen	to sink
sich unterhalten	to talk
unterschreiben	to sign
die Untertasse (-n)	saucer
die Vase (-n)	vase
der Vater (Väter)	father
Vati	Dad
sich verabschieden	to say goodbye
verbinden	to join

verbrennen	to burn
verbringen	to spend (time)
die Vergangenheit	past
vergessen	to forget
verkaufen	to sell
verkehrt herum	upside down
verlassen	to leave (a place or a person)
verlieren	to lose
vermissen	to miss (someone)
verpassen	to miss (bus, train)
verrühren	to stir, to mix
verschieden	different
verschütten	to spill
verschwinden	to disappear
versprechen	to promise
verspritzen	to splash
verstecken	to hide (something)
sich verstecken	to hide (yourself)
verstehen	to understand
versuchen	to try
viel	much, a lot
viele	many, a lot, lots
vielleicht	maybe
vier	four
viert-	fourth
das Viertel (-)	quarter
vierzehn	fourteen
vierzig	forty
violett	purple
der Vogel (Vögel)	bird
voll	full
von	from, by (done by)
vor	before, in front of
voran/gehen	to lead (go ahead)
vorbei/gehen	to pass (go past)
der, die, das Vorder-	front
die Vorderseite (-n)	front
der Vorleger (-)	rug (small)
der Vormittag (-e)	morning
wachsen	to grow (get bigger)
der Wachsmalstift (-e)	crayon
der Wagen (-)	car
wählen	to choose
wahr	true
während	while
der Wal (-e)	whale
der Wald (Wälder)	woods, forest
die Wand (Wände)	wall (inside)
wann?	when? (in questions)
warm	warm
warten	to wait
warum	why
was	what
das Waschbecken (-)	sink (bathroom)
waschen	to wash (something)
sich waschen	to wash (yourself)
die Waschmaschine (-n)	washing machine
das Wasser	water
wecken	to wake (someone)
der Wecker (-)	alarm clock
der Weg (-e)	path, way (route)
weg/nehmen	to take (away)
weh/tun	to hurt
weich	soft, smooth (skin)
die Weide (-n)	field (for animals)
Weihnachten	Xmas
weil	because
weinen	to cry
weiß	white
weit	wide, far
welcher?, welche?, welches?, welche?	which? (in questions)
die Welle (-n)	wave
die Welt	world
der Weltraum	space (outer space)
wenige	few
weniger	less
wenn	if, when
wer?	who? (in questions)
werfen	to throw
das Wetter	weather
das Wettrennen (-)	race
wichtig sein	to matter, to be important
wie	like, how, what . . . like?
wie alt	how old
wieder	again
wie viel	how much
wie viele	how many
wild	wild
der Wind (-e)	wind
winken	to wave
der Winter	winter
winzig	tiny
wirklich	real (not imaginary)
wissen	to know (facts)
der Witz (-e)	joke
wo	where
die Woche (-n)	week
wohnen	to live (somewhere), to stay (visit)
die Wolke (-n)	cloud
wollen	to want
das Wort (Wörter or Worte)	word
das Wörterbuch (Wörterbücher)	dictionary
der Wunsch (Wünsche)	wish
sich etwas wünschen	to make a wish
die Wurst (Würste)	sausage
die Wüste (-n)	desert
die Wüstenspringmaus (Wüstenspringmäuse)	gerbil
das Xylophon (-e)	xylophone
die Zahl (-en)	number (figure)
zahlen	to pay
der Zahn (Zähne)	tooth
der Zahnarzt (Zahnärzte)	dentist (man)
die Zahnärztin (-nen)	dentist (woman)
die Zahnbürste (-n)	toothbrush
die Zahnpasta	toothpaste
zart	pale (color), soft
der, die, das Zauber-	magic
die Zauberkunst	magic
der Zauberspruch (Zaubersprüche)	spell (magic)
der Zaun (Zäune)	fence
das Zebra (-s)	zebra
die Zehe (-n)	toe
zehn	ten
zehnt-	tenth
das Zeichen (-)	sign (symbol)
zeichnen	to draw
die Zeichnung (-en)	drawing
zeigen	to show, to point
die Zeit	time
die Zeitung (-en)	newspaper
das Zelt (-e)	tent
zelten	to camp
zerbrechen	to break
das Zicklein (-)	kid (baby goat)
die Ziege (-n)	goat
ziehen	to pull, to grow (cultivate)
ziemlich	quite (fairly)
das Zimmer (-)	room (in house)
die Zitrone (-n)	lemon
der Zoo (-s)	zoo
zu	to (a place), too (hot or cold)
der Zucker	sugar
zu Ende	over (finished)
zuerst	first
zu Fuß gehen	to walk, to go on foot
der Zug (Züge)	train
zu Hause	at home
zuletzt	last
zu/machen	to close, to shut
die Zunge (-n)	tongue
zusammen	together
zusammen/falten	to fold
zusammen/passen	to match
zusammen/zählen	to add (numbers)
zu/werfen	to throw (to someone)
zu/winken	to wave (to someone)
zwanzig	twenty
zwei	two
der Zweig (-e)	branch, stick
zweit-	second
die Zwiebel (-n)	onion
der Zwilling (-e)	twin
zwischen	between
zwölf	twelve

Hear the words on the Internet

If you can use the Internet and your computer can play sounds, you can listen to all the German words and phrases in this dictionary, read by a German person.

Go to the Usborne Quicklinks Website at **www.usborne-quicklinks.com** Type in the keywords **german picture dictionary** and follow the simple instructions. Try listening to the words or phrases and then saying them yourself. This will help you learn to speak German easily and well.

Always follow the safety rules on the right when you are using the Internet.

What you need

To play the German words, your computer may need a small program called an audio player, such as

RealPlayer® or Windows® Media Player. These programs are free, and if you don't already have one, you can download a copy from **www.usborne-quicklinks.com**

Internet safety rules

- Ask your parent's, guardian's or teacher's permission before you connect to the Internet.
- When you are on the Internet, never tell anyone your full name, address or telephone number, and ask an adult before you give your email address.
- If a website asks you to log in or register by typing your name or email address, ask an adult's permission first.
- If you receive an email from someone you don't know, tell an adult and do not reply to the email.

Notes for parents or guardians

The Picture Dictionary area of the Usborne Quicklinks Website contains no links to external websites. However, other areas of Usborne Quicklinks do contain links to websites that do not belong to Usborne Publishing. The links are regularly reviewed and updated, but Usborne Publishing is not responsible, and does not accept liability, for the content or availability of any website other than its own, or for any exposure to harmful,

offensive or inaccurate material which may appear on the Web.

We recommend that children are supervised while on the Internet, that they do not use Internet chat rooms and that you use Internet filtering software to block unsuitable material. Please ensure that your children follow the safety guidelines above. For more information, see the "Net Help" area on the Usborne Quicklinks Website at **www.usborne-quicklinks.com**

With thanks to Staedtler for providing the Fimo® material for models.
Bruder® toys supplied by Euro Toys and Models Ltd.
Additional models by Les Pickstock, Barry Jones, Stef Lumley, Karen Krige and Stefan Barnett
Americanization editor: Carrie Armstrong

First published in 2004 by Usborne Publishing Ltd, 83-85 Saffron Hill, London EC1N 8RT, England. www.usborne.com
Copyright © 2004 Usborne Publishing Ltd.